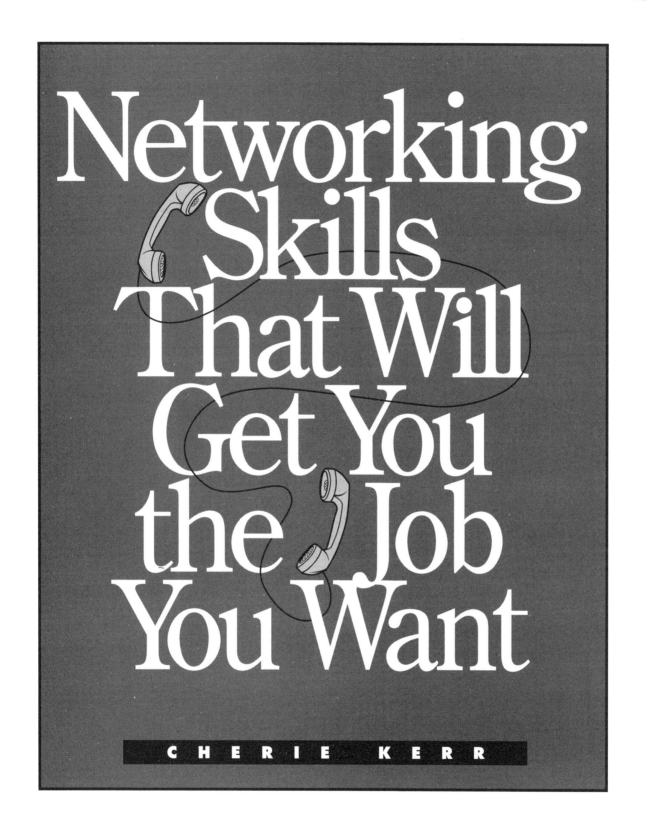

Networking Skills That Will Get You the Job You Want

CHERIE KERR

BETTERWAY BOOKS

CINCINNATI, OHIO

For Drake
—*and all the others who strive to live their dream*

"I find the great thing in this world is not so much where we stand as in what direction we are moving."

—OLIVER WENDELL HOLMES

Networking Skills That Will Get You the Job You Want.
Copyright © 1999 by Cherie Kerr. Printed and bound in the United States of America. All rights reserved. No part of this book may be reproduced in any form or by any electronic or mechanical means including information storage and retrieval systems without permission in writing from the publisher, except by a reviewer, who may quote brief passages in a review. Published by Betterway Books, an imprint of F&W Publications, Inc., 1507 Dana Avenue, Cincinnati, Ohio 45207. (800) 289-0963. First edition.

Other fine Betterway Books are available from your local bookstore or direct from the publisher.

03 02 01 00 99   5 4 3 2 1

Library of Congress Cataloging-in-Publication Data

Kerr, Cherie.
   Networking skills that will get you the job you want /
Cherie Kerr.
      p.   cm.
   Includes bibliographical references and index.
   ISBN 1-55870-501-5 (paperback : alk. paper)
   1. Job hunting. 2. Social networks. I. Title.
HF5382.7.K5   1998
650.14—dc21   98-43976
                                                CIP

Editor: David Borcherding
Production coordinator: Erin Boggs
Production editor: Jeff Crump
Interior designer: Sandy Kent
Cover designer: Kathy DeZarn

table of contents

ABOUT THE AUTHOR

Cherie Kerr is the founder and president of ExecuProv, a career networking and communications consultancy. In addition to lecturing and teaching for ExecuProv, Kerr provides speechwriting services for many of her clients. She has provided classes and private coaching to hundreds of business professionals, and her client list includes such corporations as ARCO, GTE, *Self Magazine*, Foothill Capital, Nissan Motors, Mitsubishi, Banc One, Bank of America and Casio. She has written two books: *I've Asked Miller to Say a Few Words: New and Exciting Ways to Improve Speaking and Presentation Skills Through the Use of Improvisational Comedy*, and *When I Say This, Do You Mean That . . . ? One-On-One Skills for the Business Professional*. Cherie has also been a successful actress, improv comedian and teacher, award-winning public relations head and public appearance coach.

Networking: What Is It, Anyway?

zigzagged my way through stacks of folders and notes, clearing off my desk to begin this book, and suddenly noticed that two out of every three pieces of mail I'd collected in my "read-later pile" had the word "networking" on them. One headline for a networking seminar read: "Network or No Work." Another said, "Network Your Way to Millions or Settle for What You Have Now," and a third claimed, "Networking Is the Only Bridge to the Twenty-First Century."

While all these messages seemed comically ominous, I knew that "junk" mail headlines always let the business professional know what's hot and where the industry is headed.

Reading through various materials, I realized there are all kinds of companies selling some form of networking know-how. These services—mailing lists, seminars, workshops, tapes, books and personal consulting—focus on the absolute necessity of networking. Networking isn't arbitrary anymore, these materials repeatedly point out; it is essential to surviving and thriving in the business world in the twenty-first century.

I continued to explore my cluttered desk and counted how many times I read the word "networking." I spotted it in the business journals I was tossing out, on the covers of two communications books I'd bought but had not yet read. Even a speech I was helping a client rewrite had a whole page on "networking tactics for people in the mattress manufacturing business." It was clear to me that networking is taking over every industry—every profession—in a big way.

As a public relations professional, I had been networking all my life, while never really giving much thought to the mechanics of it. Networking: What is it, exactly? To me, networking meant accessing whatever I needed to reach a goal. But this was just my interpretation. I asked a cross section of people to define "networking" and quickly realized that others had their own ideas as to what it was all about.

An outplacement-agency executive said networking is "the glue that will hold the business world together in the twenty-first century."

A journalist dubbed it the "octopus thing— it's like having tentacles in every part of the business community."

A marketing guru to the legal community said it's "assisting people to accomplish their business goals."

A political campaign manager called it "schmoozing."

An energetic secretary said, "It's back scratching in a fun way, and it never ends."

An executive at a major film studio said it is not only "getting to know people in similar fields as the ones in which you work but also expanding your base of connections daily to get to know people in completely different fields."

To one of the country's most visionary marketing strategists, networking is "exchanging information with others, always with the idea of developing long-term relationships."

The owner of an executive search and human resource development agency described it as a "process that allows us to meet people who will help us achieve our dreams and goals."

And finally, a top marketing and networking expert said, "Networking isn't just about meeting people and collecting business cards. It's about making connections in a very personal way."

Through these and other interviews, I came to understand that networking is both an art and a science. On the art side, networking requires responding to your own instincts and ideas— something we shy away from far too often in the business world. On the scientific side, it requires the constant and sometimes tedious task of gathering facts and information.

All my survey participants told me, albeit in different ways, that ultimately, *networking is about making connections.* So the adage "it's who you know" applies not just to show business but to every business. It's connections that get us from

point "A" to our final destination. Those connections lead to *other* connections. That's what networking is.

After all was said and done, I came to realize the bottom line: *Networking is an activity that enables you to access and link up to appropriate and useful connections.* Such connections can be vital to achieving a goal, whether it's finding that job from heaven or a special kind of peanut butter.

The ability to network effectively is the key to success in any business. Without good networking skills, you'll be limited as to how far you can go. The good news is that networking can be very fun and rewarding. As you might have guessed, there will also be roadblocks, but even they can be fun. I promise.

Chances are you, too, have been networking without really thinking of it in those terms. Ever throw a baby shower? Originate a football pool? Arrange the logistics for a car pool? Throw a fund-raiser? Start a Girl Scout troop? If you've done any of these things, you've networked. The task now is to take your existing networking skills, develop them even further and let them help you find that job you want. The chapters that lie ahead are designed to equip you with everything you need to sharpen your skills.

You will not only learn the art and fine mechanics of networking, you will also learn more about yourself in the process. The matters of what job you should be doing and in what industry are covered in part one, as well as how to identify your professional priorities in a personal way. After all, what's the point of going after the job you want if you don't first identify a specific goal, purpose and professional direction?

You'll get step-by-step "hands-on" activities designed to teach you about the act and the art of networking. You'll learn how to seek out and access the people you need and how to communicate with them once you find them. And you'll be instructed on how to present yourself impressively through general conversations, interviews and vis-à-vis your package of materials.

The final portion of the book provides you with tips on weighing job choices, positive ways to deal with rejection and ways to stay in the networking loop. You'll be shown how to network in a small town or a big city. There's also a chapter that addresses problems specific to first-time, second-time and old-time networkers.

Each lesson will be brought home in a personalized way with worksheets filled with questions and tasks that will get you started, down to business and on your way.

Before we begin, I want to mention just a couple of things about networking that I've learned while putting together this book—including some of the roadblocks and red flags.

First, networking can sometimes be boring and exhausting; that's just the nature of it. (I, personally, have had days when I felt as though I was crossing a desert without a camel.) As you engage in the networking process, you'll need to keep three basic principles firmly in mind: determination, creativity and perseverance. If any one of these fundamental tenets are not part of your mind-set, your efforts will most likely fall short of your networking goals.

The three principles were integral to the origin of this book. Out of sheer need, I had to push the limits of my creativity and use my imagination to its fullest in selecting good sources. Because I was operating out of my normal range of contacts, I had to allow myself to be free and open to a myriad of possibilities.

I had to be persistent; I had to decide from the outset that I would not forsake my goal, no matter how weary or frustrated I became. There were times when I felt like I was networking all by myself or spinning in a giant, meaningless circle. People wouldn't return calls, or when they did, their answers were vague or hard to translate into usable form. In those cases, I had to exercise my communication skills to persuade my interviewees to become interested in my project.

The most important lesson for me, though, was that I had to stay on top of this project with an unrelenting zeal. That's the hardest part—the follow-through. It's fairly easy to bolt out of the gate with a burst of mental and physical energy, but maintaining the stamina and fortitude to pursue a goal all the way to the finish line is something else entirely.

Despite networking being such a part of daily life, many people lack the confidence to network in the business world. They are so afraid of brick walls, rejection and new horizons that they stay unhappily stuck. To those people—in fact, to everyone interested in improving their networking skills—I recommend reading *The Little Engine That Could* by Watty Piper. Its overall message is the subtext of this book.

Networking, in the end, is all about relationships and nothing but relationships. It was the one recurring theme I found with everyone I talked to. So if you're not one for meeting new people, you're going to have to overcome your shyness. If you do like meeting new people, be certain you make more time for it. I know that's hard in this fast-paced, highly technological world we live in. We lack time, and relationships take time to establish, maintain and nurture. But establishing rapport with others and building on that rapport is fundamental to the concept of networking. I call this "working the loop." That's the basic meaning of networking: making connections and building relationships.

Enough explanation of what networking is; now let's go do it.

chapter one

A Positive ID

Before we delve into the how-to's of networking, you need to be clear on where you want to go occupationally. After all, what's the point of networking if you're not guiding yourself in the right direction? That would be like shopping in a hardware store for a pair of shoes. To gain more clarity, take a close look at what you want to be doing. How to go about that? Scrutinize what you're really good at. We're all good at something. In fact, we're all great at something. Here's a thought: You might want to tackle this assignment by going at it backward, by making a list of what you're not good at doing. (For instance, I could never be a chef. But that's okay, I'd rather buy clothes than pans any day.)

THE KEY TO YOU

What you're good at is your key to professional happiness, success and fulfillment—the key to you. What comes easily and naturally is what you should be doing in the workplace. Unfortunately, too many business professionals are doing some-

thing other than what they really want to do.

If you are one of the many who don't have a clue what you want to do or where you want to go, or worse yet, you're off on some unfulfilling professional tangent, you need to take a close look at your likes and dislikes.

I'm going to ask you to answer some pretty specific questions later in this chapter. In so doing, you may reaffirm what you already know. You may also be surprised at what you discover about yourself as well as your untapped career capabilities. You just may end up wanting to make some changes.

MAKING UP YOUR MIND

I get crazy when I hear adults ask children: "And what do you want to *be* when you grow up?" The answer should be an adjective like "happy," not a noun like "fireman." But as youngsters we're programmed early on by being asked this question. We're compelled to be something that we're not supposed to be.

For those who are not absolutely sure "what

you want to be when you grow up," this chapter will help you pinpoint a number of possible career choices you may have overlooked. It is designed to help you focus on your specific skills and show you how to put them into action to realize your career potential.

And if you don't identify with the aforementioned group, this section is geared toward getting you moving in a more definitive and appropriate direction.

Perhaps you're one of those business professionals who is ready to move forward into another field, but you're not sure which. Again, the questions put forth later in this chapter will help you solidify a hunch or two.

This is not to say you should only focus on innate skills; you should hang on to your dreams and make every effort to live them out. That's one of the biggest problems each of us encounters—going for what is practical rather than what is possible. We often don't listen to our gut feelings. A strong inkling is often the magnetic force pulling us toward our dreams. But how many times have you chosen to ignore one of those tugs in exchange for "making a living."

As you proceed along this part of the journey, hold on to those dreams, and pay attention to your hunches.

THREE LITTLE WORDS

Remember the three basic principles of networking: determination, creativity and perseverance. You can apply this trio when considering what you should be doing. You should be determined to find the answer, creative enough to explore all possibilities that scream "that's me," and then persevere like an offensive lineman to find opportunities that fit your personal identity and complement your passion and talent.

Bill Ellermeyer, of Lee Hecht Harrison (a job-outplacement center), tells his charges to recall what talents and abilities they seemed to come by effortlessly as young children. Bill maintains that such realizations often ignite that flame of job passion. He believes that what we wanted to do, or what we did well as kids, leads us toward a viable career path and that we should follow those initial blueprints.

PUTTING YOUR FINGER ON IT

Some people spend their lives hopping from job to job in the aimless pursuit of trying out things. Others simply find a job and stay in it for a sense of security until the "right job comes along."

I say nuts to both those philosophies. You don't have to spend years floundering in the job search or stuck in a lousy job to finally pinpoint what it is you want to do. Simple answers to simple questions will help you shortcut that frustration.

It's possible to identify a professional passion early on and launch yourself into the business world from a standpoint of strength. This doesn't mean you won't change jobs or even careers throughout your professional life. Quite the contrary. Most truly successful business people change careers three to five times in their lives or at least explore different aspects of their chosen professions. I'm referring to people who grow through career changes—people who transition from plateau to plateau through similar jobs to reach their passionate goal—because that journey is often most rewarding. Usually this group has some grasp on what they're suited for from the beginning. They just continue to stack up those building blocks while they gain skills and rack up accomplishments. Those are the types who acquire what it takes to finally hit their career pinnacle.

Unfortunately, too many talented people

become "job hoppers." They launch themselves into one job, then another, with equal amounts of enthusiasm and drive until they hit a blockade. Then they are back at the starting line to take off for yet another exciting job possibility. They never really get anywhere meaningful, or if they do, they take years to finally hit their mark—sometimes by sheer luck, not necessarily skill. Job hoppers gain little to take with them to the next destination, while the career changer is one who adds what she has gained to the next job experience.

Career changers are business professionals who, throughout their career, may change occupations three to five times to experience their full potential. They are not the same as those who carelessly wander from job to job and feel their way around with no real objective in mind.

Then there are some who never get anywhere—who have never assessed their talents. They haven't gotten in touch with what they are really cut out to do. They just stay in a ho-hum kind of existence.

It's all right to change jobs because you're expanding and growing in your field, and it's OK to hit and miss a few times while you get a better grasp on your career direction. However, not exploring your true skills and deep passions is a great personal loss.

HOW MUCH ARE YOU WILLING TO RISK?

One of the most heartbreaking experiences in my professional career has been to watch many of my friends waste their productive years in jobs they hated or not pursue the ones they really wanted. None of us should have to look back and regret what we have done with our lives.

I'm big on taking chances. Without them you miss out on life. That's not to say you should be reckless or careless, but if you want to realize your dreams, you need to seek and explore. And you are no exception: You have innate talents and deep-seated passions. As you make your personal positive identification, I challenge you to lean over the edge of what's comfortable. When you think about it, what do you have to lose? One way to manage your risk factor is to pursue your passion on the side; moonlighting is a great way to build confidence, skill and financial momentum. It's also a great way to find something that resonates with you.

Before we network our way towards the job we want, we have to look carefully within ourselves to square off with our passion and our innate talent. We need to recognize and appreciate what we're here to do. And I believe we're all here to contribute something meaningful to the society in which we live.

So ask the following: What are my dreams worth to me? Am I really losing anything by moonlighting for a time in my "dream" profession? How much risk is too much? What exactly am I willing to risk—lifestyle, prestige, status, money? If I risk these now, can I have them later if I hit my mark? What's the worst that can happen if I take the risk to do what I really want to do, professionally?

If you're skittish about taking risks, take a calculated one and moonlight for a time—get a side job, weekends or nights—and check out what you perceive to be your dream job. You have nothing to lose except time, but I believe such time will be well spent. You can rule out what isn't "you," and you can test out what might be. Moonlighting also allows you to explore more than one area of interest before you delve into a job.

WHAT'S SCHOOL GOT TO DO WITH IT?

Nothing is more valuable than a good education to help you get the job you want. But education is only a small part of the bigger picture. Without passion and talent for a particular occupation, even a dozen degrees won't make you truly qualified. You might end up with the right amount of education, but you may not be happy regardless of your status, power or money. And getting the job you want equates with happiness and fulfillment. Why should we settle for less when we spend most of our lives on the job? And life really is so short.

While conducting the poll I discussed in the introduction, I talked to several midlevel executives who felt trapped in jobs they truly disliked—the very jobs they had spent their education preparing for. Most of the college graduates I polled said what they majored in had no connection with what they really loved doing. They did it for Mom, Dad or potential bucks. Later they regretted not following or even examining their talents and passions.

Many business professionals I talked to who didn't satisfy their passions and talents felt they had wasted precious years—some, entire careers. In hindsight, they wished they had placed less emphasis on getting grades and more on lifelong career satisfaction. They ended up commiserating with fellow colleagues over what they should have done professionally.

If you're in that boat, jump ship now and go where you were destined to go. If you're just starting out, let this be a warning.

One way to find out if you're headed in the right direction is to answer my first big question: What did you fall in love with academically? Question number two: Are you presently doing anything connected to it for a living?

TRUE CONFESSIONS

I'm probably the best case study I know when it comes to proving the Ellermeyer theory—to do in adulthood what seemed effortless to you as a child—because I ended up doing what I loved and what I had a predilection for. As a youngster, I thrived on playacting and making up stories and plays. I would act them out or write them down. I studied theater from age four to eleven. But here's the sad twist. During adolescence, I moved to a new city and met a new group of friends with very different interests. In my quest for approval, I put my deep-down, burning aspirations on hold. My focus became making friends and gaining acceptance. Sometimes teenagers believe being part of a group is more important than anything else. Some carry that need into adulthood. It's just the way many learn to function in the world. I fell into that category for a time.

It wasn't until my junior year in high school that I finally became interested in any class, and that class was literature. I should have listened to that inkling more carefully. It certainly dovetailed nicely into my prekindergarten interests of writing plays. I should have known then what direction I should be headed, but I took the long way around.

Two years into college I decided to get married. Six years later (after two children), I divorced. I had no full college education to fall back on, no real workplace skills and though I needed a job, I had very little experience. I applied for the position of receptionist/telephone operator for a home building company that was also looking to hire a public relations person. When my soon-to-be boss asked if I could write, I spontaneously stretched the truth and said, "yes." He was interviewing me for both jobs, apparently. I felt relatively sure I would get the phone job and was shocked when he called and told me I had the PR position. I didn't know whether to tell him I had no real writing experience or just wait to be fired; I decided to play the waiting game. I figured I had nothing to lose and went for it. I worked hard during the day, faking it for the first few months. At night I dashed home and studied every possible periodical and magazine in an attempt to train myself in Associated Press writing style, PR writing style and every other writing style known to man. Everything with words on it suddenly became a focus of study; I even became intrigued with the way verbiage was tightly organized on a clothing label. I did all this while feeding, bathing and playing with two children under the age of three.

I was simultaneously tired, frantic and euphoric. Like Anne Boelyn, I felt my head might roll at any time; unlike Anne, I felt I deserved it. But I was working hard and loving it, and soon my boss was effusive about my work. Within a year I had won several copywriting awards for my efforts. (It all came so easy for me.) Shortly thereafter I was hired by the company's ad agency to work in their budding public relations department. My four-year stint there was like a college education, and I worked hard to acquire all the skills to be both a writer and a promoter of special events. Through my work as a special-event coordinator, incidentally, I became a consummate networker.

I did several PR-related jobs over the next few years, including freelance writing for magazines. A short time later I became a freelance publicist for several entrepreneurs. One thing led to another, I started my own public relations firm, had twenty people on staff at its peak and won a bunch of awards. I was getting to do what I loved—writing, promoting, networking—all the while capitalizing on my innate talents and my deepest passions.

What about the playacting? Well, that was another avocation getting sated. In my early days at the ad agency, I joined the L.A. Groundlings, a group that went on to become one of the foremost sketch and improv groups in the country. There is not a sitcom, feature film or show on the air that doesn't have an L.A. Groundling attached to it in some way. Many of its alumni went on to *Saturday Night Live.* I have my own sketch and improv group in Orange County, the Crazies, and a profitable company, ExecuProv, that teaches presentation and communication skills to business executives, using improv comedy techniques as the fundamental teaching theory. (I also help these people write speeches.) This work has satisfied yet another childhood dream.

I share all this with you because it illustrates the point I was making earlier: If you tap into your "beginnings" and use your basic talent, you're bound to be successful. In fact, I believe it's impossible to fail. Granted, I studied along the way (I still do), and I worked very, very hard. But working hard isn't hard when you love the process.

I'm one of those people I mentioned earlier—I grew from one professional experience into another, branching out and expanding to incorporate all I am good at and all that I love.

So as you clarify what you really want to do, check out what you *like* to do. Take stock of what you're good at. Therein lies the answer to identifying your professional potential. One last note: When you do the personal inventory quiz on page 10, forget about money, status, fame, recognition and prestige. Oftentimes the quest for these payoffs keeps you from ever realizing your potential or allowing you to come face-to-face with your deep-down dreams.

Here's another great yardstick: If you're doing what you enjoy as a job task and have no idea how much time has passed—if you are so immersed in what you're doing that you don't care about time—that's one indicator of what you probably should be doing. When I'm writing or rehearsing a show, I have no idea what time it is. Furthermore, I don't care. That tells me I'm working at exactly what I should be working at.

Interpreting Your Answers

After compiling your answers to the quiz, you should notice a common thread in many of your responses. In fact, your answers should repeat a specific theme. The most important question is: Does the overriding theme match the occupation you listed in question number 20? If so, then you're probably where you want to be. You may still need to explore that field you're in. Do you want to go further in it? Sidestep into a related field?

If the answer to number 20 does not coincide with your other answers, it's time to reassess your career direction, regardless of your age or professional status. It's also time to plug into sources where you can further explore your career aptitude. (Refer to chapter two, "Exploring Suitable Job Opportunities," and chapter three, "Beyond Job Description." They will be a big help.)

The whole point of the questionnaire and homework assignments is to clearly identify your professional potential and to find out whether or not you are exactly where you want to be as a business professional, or if you're even close. If the answer is "no," then you still have work to do. Helping you find your way to those answers is part of this book's purpose.

MATCHING YOUR INTERESTS TO SPECIFIC CAREER FIELDS

The following exercises are designed to help you clarify and identify your professional potential. They will steer you toward specific fields that are "friendly" to a person with your interests and abilities. They are also designed to help you access workplace opportunities to realize even greater career satisfaction.

1. Contact an employment agency, college counseling center or career-outplacement facility and ask for tests to help pinpoint your potential strengths and weaknesses. Take a test. In fact, take several. A good cross section will be very revealing.

2. Call your mother, father, brothers or sisters. Take notes as they recall the special abilities and gifts you had as a child.

3. If possible, contact your favorite high school or college teacher and see what advice and encouragement they can give you regarding your career choice. This applies even if you are a business executive or have been in a job ten years or more. Some of those teachers can still be found and most will remember you. Ask specifically what impressed them about your potential.

4. If you have identified what you would really like to do, visit companies in that field. To find such companies, ask colleagues, friends and neighbors. Call ahead to see if you can visit their facility and learn more about their daily work assignments and activities. Explore colleges, trade schools and trade organizations, as well as companies that host workshops and seminars in the field that intrigues you. Learn all you can—at least enough to land a job that would launch a career in your dream field.

If you're a major executive and you simply want to take your skills to an industry you love, check out that industry and get as much

THE QUIZ: YOUR PERSONAL INVENTORY

Answer these questions as honestly and spontaneously as you can. After taking this test, please do the subsequent homework, as it will aid you in developing your innate talents.

1. As a child I was often complimented for my ability to _____
    I first recall getting such a compliment when I was _____ years old.
2. I hated it when I had to stop playing _____
3. As a child, I could be engaged in the following activity for hours and never become bored:
    _____
4. When I was little and I daydreamed about doing something, it was always about
    _____
5. _____ was hard for some kids, but it was always easy for me.
6. The famous people I always admired as a child were _____
    I admired them because _____
7. When I was a little I said I wanted to grow up to be an _____
8. When I role-played or playacted, it was in the following scenarios: _____
    _____
9. When I did _____ I never gave much thought about how to do it.
10. If I could do anything as a business professional, it would be _____
    _____
11. At my current job, I really enjoy _____
12. In terms of chores, tasks or jobs to date, _____
    has been my absolute favorite (even if it was a part-time or summer job).
13. In junior high or high school, I suddenly became interested in _____
14. In college I majored in ____ . (Circle one) A) I was glad I had. (B) At some point I realized I
    was interested in something else. C) I wished I had majored in _____
    instead.
15. In terms of a career choice, my parents tried to persuade me to pursue A) Something that
    paid well. B) Something I really loved. C) Both. D) None of the above.
16. The business professional who I know personally and most admire is _____
    His or her job is _____
17. I always end up in job-related situations where my ability to _____
    comes in handy.
18. The people close to me are always saying, "You should go into the field of _____
    _____," or "You should be a
    _____"
19. I would rather do _____ for a living than what I am doing now.
20. My current occupation is _____

information as you can from the contacts you have. For example, you may be a real estate developer and wish to be a film producer. Their actual job responsibilities don't differ greatly; if you can do one you can do the other. Begin to get a realistic sense of the field you wish to transfer to, lining up your prospective employers. Deciding how to package and pitch yourself will be covered in subsequent chapters.

5. Keep a daily journal of interesting industries you've become exposed to. Television magazine programs, the news and talk shows often feature unique people and their jobs. *Time*, *Newsweek*, *People* and other weekly periodicals also highlight different individuals, their occupations and their success stories. Such homework not only helps you identify your area or areas of interest, it also provides terrific inspiration and encouragement for following your own dreams.

6. Make a list of your favorite positive affirmations and post them where you will see them often. Look for things to remind you that you're special and different and have something unusual and individual to share with the world. Sometimes we forget we're all here for specific reasons.

7. Go back and review your report cards if you still have them. What you scored well on may give you some key answers as to what you're really good at. Write the subjects down and compare them with what you're doing and what you want to do.

If you take time to hone in on what you like to do, you'll undoubtedly hit upon what it is you *should* do. Again, there is no point in beginning the networking process until you know where you want to go.

chapter two

Exploring Suitable Job Opportunities

Now that you've identified your passions and talents to get a better feel for what you should be doing professionally, let's explore the career opportunities that might be a good match for you. As you begin this exploration, you'll find yourself energetically networking because the way you make a selection takes a fair amount of networking skill. So it's time to partner up your gifts and interests. Shortly, you'll learn how to put all this into action to land the job you truly want.

PLANNING YOUR EXPEDITION

As you go about the exploration process, there will be times when you'll feel overwhelmed with information; it may come at you fast and furious, so keeping it carefully organized is a must. Your first task is to set up a practical filing system. Your first file: "Me and the Job I Want." That's where you'll put your preliminary notes, those scraps of paper where you jotted down an idea, a to-do task or the name of a contact who might provide answers or insight in your search for the ideal job.

Staying organized is crucial to your search. It's too easy to become confused and flustered when you have bits of paper scattered everywhere, so grab those things you carelessly tossed in your purse, briefcase, car glovebox or junk drawer, and put them in appropriate files. As you weigh and consider the job possibilities you're likely to discover during this freewheeling expedition, you'll appreciate being able to refer back to information without having to search your entire house to find it. Think of it like a sock drawer: If you throw them all in one drawer, at least you'll know where to go to get socks. Later, you can organize your files so the information is paired appropriately. If you don't have a filing cabinet, you can purchase an inexpensive cardboard file box at an office supply store.

The point is that having info ready, categorized and easily retrievable will save you hours later and will make assimilating information much easier. This is important when making a life decision such as "what career is for me," because you'll want to be as objective as possible. Good organization will help you make informed and objective choices. I'm not asking you to become so compulsive that you drive everyone around you nuts; I'm just asking that you discipline yourself so you can get off to a great start.

THE GATHERING PROCESS

Once you've established a system for staying organized, you can begin gathering more information. Look for anything that chronicles your fields of interest. Gather:

- magazine and newspaper articles
- brochures and annual reports
- audio and video interviews (or transcripts of them)
- notes from conversations with experts in your potential fields
- reports (summaries in your own words) on your research efforts
- Web sites and other Internet resources
- titles of books that bring you up to speed on the trends of the industry or that provide additional information, education or insight about the field you've chosen.

This gathering process also includes pulling together all those random scraps of paper you have laying around.

Make a master file for information that relates very broadly to your field of interest. For example, if you're interested in the hospitality industry, you'd make a master file called "Hospitality." As you research the field, you'll probably discover that it has a variety of subfields. Make a file for each, for example, "Restaurants," "Hotels," "Resorts," "Spas," "Food Catering" and "Special-Event Planning."

Let's say you want to delve further into the subcategory "Restaurants." Files under that heading might include "Restaurant Chains," "Fast-Food Franchises," "Upscale Dinner Houses," "Specialty or Themed Restaurants" and so on. The key is to make a master file and secondary files for each category worthy of exploration. These additional files are designed to help you subdivide and keep track of your information. Take this idea a step further: If you continue to explore, you find yourself especially interested in "Specialty or Themed Restaurants." You might make additional subfiles such as "Hard Rock Cafe," "Planet Hollywood," "Medieval Times," "Chuck E. Cheese" and so forth.

I cannot stress enough the importance of keeping information organized. In my own work, it has been invaluable. I'm the kind of person who is always ripping out magazine articles (don't tell my dentist) that contain tidbits of information I think will be useful in my books, speeches, training seminars or satirical revues. Without my files, I would spend hours trying to locate that one great piece of information I suddenly needed. Some discipline is a great habit to get into, no matter how long you've been a member of the workforce. If you end up investigating several industries before you hit upon the right one, it's all the more important that your files are in order.

Let's assume your answers to the quiz in chapter one indicate that advertising is your field of interest. Let's assume further that you have a particular penchant for the more creative aspects of the field. You'll want to identify the tasks performed daily in the advertising agency environment. And, of course, you'll want to keep track of this information by means of an orderly filing system. Your master file will be "Advertising," and your next file will be "Creative Jobs in Advertising." From there you'll subdivide further. Your first subfile under "Creative Jobs" might be "Copywriter," followed by "Creative Director," "Graphic Designer," "Illustrator," etc.

You can also go about your expedition in another way. Let's say you know you want to be in a job that involves accounting. You may want to explore the different industries that fascinate you in order to put your skills into practice as an accountant, an industry that clearly meets your criteria in terms of talents and passions. So even though you may be doing the research process backwards, you get the same outcome. You may be interested in looking into the entertainment, political, legal or sports fields as they relate to accounting positions. Your master file would read "Accountant," and your subfiles would be categorized into industries of interest.

Gather as much information as possible for every position that intrigues you. You'll especially want to investigate the day-to-day job responsibilities of the position. After all, it's what's required day in and day out that will help determine whether or not the job you think you want is, in fact, right for you.

You certainly don't want to waste time networking your way into a job that doesn't meet your personal and professional standards, or more importantly, doesn't match your passions and talents. Remember, the idea of your exploration is to get a hands-on, in-depth, realistic look at your area of interest.

TALK ISN'T CHEAP

Now that you're clear on what you wish to explore and you have your filing system in place, it's time to talk to as many people as possible who do the jobs that interest you. This gives you the opportunity to thoroughly consider if their jobs—their *real* world—match your goals and career fantasies. You don't want to heavily pur-

sue a field of interest without first finding out all you can about it. On the surface, many jobs may sound fascinating, but in reality they may be boring to you or they may not utilize your full potential.

Whatever field you choose to investigate, make that search thorough. There are often many aspects to a particular field. Some jobs look glamorous and exciting on the surface but turn out to have day-to-day responsibilities that don't suit you. I have a friend who wanted to be a television news anchor. As he got into the news business, he soon found that editing was far more appealing. I have another friend who plays character roles in major feature films and sitcoms. She can be on a set for ten hours before she's called before the camera, but she has such a passion for her work that she doesn't mind. Would you?

As you do this part of the exploration process, keep in mind that none of your time will be wasted; every interview provides more information and insight, which is truly what you're after. You may talk to ten people in the advertising industry, and through that series of interviews, learn that there is one common aspect of that industry that wouldn't work for you or one that really makes you want to go for it. For example, irregular hours are typical in the advertising business. Some people work all weekend just to finish a campaign for a Monday morning pitch. I don't know too many people who ever do this type of work nine to five. Talking to a good cross section of people is wise so you can get a vivid picture of what their industry is all about and exactly what their jobs entail. On the other hand, you may find that 90 percent of their job involves imagination and that the desire to use your creativity outweighs having to work overtime.

WHERE DO YOU FIND THEM?

If you don't already know some people, or if you don't have friends or associates who can refer you to specific sources, look in newspapers, magazines and other trade journals to find names of people who fit your field of interest. In either case, call or write to those you wish to interview and ask if you can talk to them about their respective jobs. Assure them that you know their time is valuable. Offer to buy them lunch, a cup of coffee or a drink if their schedule permits. Many people appreciate such a gesture in exchange for their time and input.

If they only have time for a telephone interview, thank them and keep your interview short and to the point. Most people don't mind taking time to answer your questions if you're well prepared and have a handful of specific questions to ask them. Be clear about what you want to know.

WHAT TO ASK

As you start your interviews, make sure you have a written list of questions that you want to ask—questions that are direct and to the point. Take plenty of time to make your notes. Did you cover everything? After your time with these people, you don't want to have any regrets, and you don't want to keep bugging someone for "just one more thing." I suggest asking:

1. What hours do you work?
2. Please give me a brief overview of your daily job responsibilities.
3. What do you like most about your job?
4. What type of skills and background would I need to do your job?
5. What classes, workshops or seminars would best equip me for your job?
6. What do you dislike most about your job?
7. How does your job relate to what it is you really want to do?
8. Why did you get into this field?
9. How did you get into this field?
10. What is your background?
11. Where did you study? What classes did you take?
12. If you don't mind my asking, what kind of money do you make?
13. What do you think the future would bring if I pursued a job in this field?
14. If you had it to do over again, would you pursue the same career? If not, what would you have done?
15. What advantages have been added to your life because of the job you do?
16. Can you tell me more about the industry in general?

The last question is essential. For instance, if you were talking to people in health care, you may learn that there are major concerns about the industry's future due to managed health care programs. Getting a slant on the future is important; you don't want to link up with an industry that may be facing some tough times.

The following are other ways to ascertain information as you go about the exploration process.

CLASSES AND SEMINARS

There are places you can go to study for every industry. You may want to investigate the entertainment industry, for example. You can contact local clubs and groups to inquire what seminars and workshops are available. If you don't know names of specific groups who sponsor such events, here are some ways to make headway.

1. Call friends who know someone in your area of interest, and see what information they have about clubs and associations that host events.

2. Pick up any trade publication for that industry and call their editorial staff. They will always be able to provide leads on groups who sponsor and provide workshops and seminars.

3. Look on the Internet or the World Wide Web, and select a category that offers information to lead you in the right direction. Another way to use the Internet is to put out a blanket request to a chat room to see if anyone can provide a referral.

4. Contact your local career-guidance center and ask them for a referral. Most every city has some type of career center. If not, contact your local college or school that provides extension courses, and see what they have available or who they know industry-wise that offers courses.

TRENDS AND THE FUTURE OF YOUR INDUSTRY

Research the trends, predictions and projections of where your industry of interest is headed in the next five, ten and twenty years. This task is one of the most important because those who are a few beats ahead of where the business community is going are the people who really cash in. Look at Bill Gates and some of the other computer-age pioneers. They were always thinking years ahead. Guess what? They still are.

You will probably meet people through workshops and seminars who can help you access such information. Most people who teach classes have a good grasp on their industry and where it is headed. They also seem to know if there are any big changes about to occur. Ask to speak to an instructor after class for lunch or a drink, and see what insight he can provide. Most teachers have statistics—numbers of all kinds that talk about the demographics of the industry's customers, the profession's probable growth, recent percentage of expansion, where and how much it grew, where it's going and so on. Getting a few minutes to ask some pointed questions or posing them during a Q&A session is one way to learn more about the industry.

Another great way to find out about trends is to contact any specialty editor of a newspaper or magazine. If you contact *Money* magazine, for instance, their estate-planning editor could easily tell you what types of living trusts are being developed for the future. An editor of *Homebuyer's Guide* could tell you what housing starts might be on the horizon in the next five years. If you're thinking about becoming an estate-planning attorney or a general contractor, these publications would give you some terrific information on how active those industries are going to be and where they may experience the most growth.

Any college can provide you with PhDs who are researching trends and developments, including medical or business schools or the arts. It just depends on what you're trying to find. Any university is a great starting point when it comes to getting information about the future or places you can contact that will provide that.

Also, there are companies who do nothing but predict trends in business. A woman by the name of Faith Popcorn has a company in New York City that consults with Fortune 500 companies about where their industries are going. Her work was critically acclaimed in the 1980s, and she created a trend for other companies to provide similar services to huge corporations. It was Popcorn who predicted the boom of the sport utility vehicle. John Naisbitt, author of a best-selling book in the 1980s called *Megatrends*, also consults with companies and helps them to understand where their industries are going.

If you're not sure how to locate one of these trend-prediction companies, call the public relations department of any Fortune 500 company like General Motors or Nabisco. They will have a list of such groups who specialize in your area of interest, and they will gladly share it with you.

READ ALL ABOUT IT

Go to a bookstore or library and gather as many books as you can that provide information on your occupation of interest. Both are filled with how-to books. Recent years have produced a plethora of books on virtually every job and industry. Every occupation has something written about it, so browse your local bookstore or library—you will be surprised at what you find.

Most of the larger bookstore chains, such as Barnes & Noble or Borders, have helpful salespeople to assist you in your search for information about any area of interest. If you can't find a section that addresses your need, don't be afraid to ask. They're used to that.

These bookstores have extensive sections on business and racks of magazines and trade journals full of valuable, current information.

Should you choose the library to access information, allow enough time to dig for it. I find that books are not as accessible in libraries as they are in bookstores. Besides that, it's just too quiet in the library. In a bookstore, I inevitably find another patron I can chat with about what I'm looking for, and I don't have to whisper!

SPREADING THE WORD

The first thing you'll want to do with all the information you've gathered is to put it in carefully labeled file folders. After all this discovery, you want to make certain to record and store your findings. Before filing things away, make diary entries and notes on your perceptions and point

of view about what you've found: the industry, the jobs tasks you've investigated, what you would enjoy and what you would not about that industry and its jobs. Similarly, make notes based on the information you gleaned from classes, workshops and seminars that provided in-depth information about your fields of interest.

Make files for all those books, trade publications, contact names and people who granted you interviews. All this will make for the beginnings of a great resource center. It's information you may want to refer to throughout your career. For instance, if you took a class called "Interior Design: How to Break Into the Industry," your brochures and notes will serve as reminders as you seek employment. They will also refresh your memory on how to approach potential employers and what they're looking for in a job candidate.

Keep detailed notes on the salient aspects of each of the above—the sum of each expedition. In other words, keep track of what stands out about your findings. Consider the relevance of these findings with respect to your talents and passions. Don't lose sight of that. If the match isn't there, start again and go through the process until you find one. Your search may seem arduous at times, but this exercise is terribly important.

Consider how much fun you'll have during this part of your discovery process. You'll learn about things you never would have known about otherwise! Personally, I think that's one of the most exhilarating aspects of all—learning things about the business world you never knew existed. There is a phrase often used in the study of improvisational comedy: Heighten and explore. Teachers will tell their students to "heighten and explore," whether it's about another actor in the scene or an invisible, imaginary object they're using in the scene. The

WORKSHEET ONE: PINPOINT THE JOB

1. Based on an inner search to determine my talents and passion, I learned that the field of _____ is where I belong.

2. Within the field of _____ , the jobs that intrigue and fascinate me most are:

   A) _____

   B) _____

   C) _____

3. For each of those jobs, the following are the job responsibilities and tasks I feel

   A) match my passion _____

   B) fit my talent _____

4. The following are things about that job I

   A) don't find appealing _____

   B) don't think I would want to do _____

   C) would most enjoy doing on a day-to-day basis _____

   _____

5. People to contact who do the jobs in which I'm interested or who could steer me to those who do:

   A) _____

   B) _____

   C) _____

6. My master file is _____

7. My subfiles include:

   A) _____

   B) _____

   C) _____

8. Books, magazines, newspapers, Web sites and resource centers where I can easily access more information about my area of professional interest include:

   A) _____

   B) _____

   C) _____

9. Classes, workshops, seminars, tapes and other materials I can attend to become more informed about or skilled at what I'd like to do:

   A) _____

   B) _____

   C) _____

10. I have made the commitment to pursue a job as a _____ because I truly believe it best meets and satisfies my talents, passions and professional needs.

WORKSHEET TWO: PINPOINT THE INDUSTRY

1. I know my job should be _____

2. I know this is the right occupation for me because it matches my talents and passions for

   _____

3. The industries that most fascinate me:

   A) _____

   B) _____

   C) _____

4. Companies at which to inquire about job openings in my area of interest:

   A) _____

   B) _____

   C) _____

5. Individuals who could provide a blow-by-blow description of the pros and cons of doing my
   job in the industries that interest me:

   A) _____

   B) _____

   C) _____

6. My master file is _____

7. My subfiles include:

   A) _____

   B) _____

   C) _____

8. Classes, workshops, seminars, tapes and other materials that would help me learn more about
   the industries that interest me:

   A) _____

   B) _____

   C) _____

9. Publications and trade journals that feature people in my intended line of work as well as
   how-to tips on doing the job well:

   A) _____

   B) _____

   C) _____

10. I have decided the field of _____

    is where I want to work as a _____

teachers believe there is no limit and no end to discovery when it comes to people and things on stage. We can apply that to our own self-discovery as we study the different fields we may want to work in. We find out so much about ourselves during our exploration travels.

Experts say we use less than 10 percent of our brainpower. What you find in your explorations may tap your mental potential and expose you to professional possibilities you never considered before.

WORKSHEETS: AN ORIENTATION

The previous worksheets were designed to help you explore potential job choices. Worksheet One covered questions for those who've pinpointed the industry they want to work in. Worksheet Two was designed for those who know the occupation they'd like to pursue, but haven't yet identified a particular industry. Here again, it's essential you keep your field organized and accessible. As you answered the questions, you may have pored over your notes and findings to provide appropriate answers. Don't forget that

the answers to these questions act as a foundation. They will build the momentum necessary to lead you toward the job you want. These worksheets will help you clarify your thoughts on paper.

TWO BIRDS, ONE STONE

All this research and interviewing counts as networking. It takes skill to ask around and research possibilities. It also takes perseverance, creativity and determination to complete the worksheet questions with answers that make sense.

By doing all the previous assignments, you'll prime yourself beautifully for the more intricate process of networking, the part that calls for accessing contacts who can help you get the job you want—the people who know the people you need to know. These assignments also require a great deal of discipline to get your information in order and set up a system to serve as the basis for your personal resource center. You'll be building on that center in a variety of ways as you walk along the networking trail.

chapter three

Beyond Job Descriptions

While a large part of your exploration thus far has had to do with looking closely at what field you're suited to, it is also important for you to look within yourself to clarify your needs, your preferences and your goals. Only then will you be able to pinpoint your professional direction. There's no point in beginning the networking process without handling these basics; you've got to know where you're headed before you set out to go there.

With that idea in mind, you'll want to assess both your short- and long-term career goals, and figure out what it will take to achieve them. You'll also want to decide whether you want to be self-employed or work for someone else, perhaps a large company or a corporation. Establishing personal priorities not only gives you something specific to aim for, but it also helps lay the groundwork for a satisfying career that evolves and grows in a meaningful way.

THE NEAR FUTURE: SHORT-TERM GOALS

Taking a close look at where you currently are and where you want to be in a short period of time is a great starting point for identifying your personal priorities. In addition to choosing the job, the location, an acceptable salary and being comfortable about the job responsibilities, you need to pinpoint and list some short-term goals. For instance, do you want a promotion within three months? Do you want your first position to be one that can easily lead to others? Do you want more money within three months? Six months? A corner office? You'd be surprised at some of the items I've seen on short-term goal lists (like the guy who wanted his name on a parking space next to the company president's), but there's no right or wrong way to make your list—what's important is to define your expectations.

I've made short-terms goals in the past that helped me clarify my needs and expectations. Just because I'm self-employed doesn't mean I don't play the same game. I make such a list with every new assignment I take on. If the short-term goals on my list aren't satisfied through my experiences, I need to switch gears and do something else. When my short-term goals are out of line with my overall goals, I'm setting myself up for frustration and possibly a disappointing detour in my career growth.

There are four basic conflicts in life: man against man, man against nature, man against society and man against himself. The latter category is the toughest to deal with. You certainly don't want to be at odds with yourself; it takes too much energy. Save that fuel for something more gratifying. Each of us should have attainable goals that move us forward. What are yours?

One way to answer that question is to make a list of what you hope to achieve in the next six months. Be exact. Don't forget to account for things that aren't exactly work related, like time off to enjoy your wedding. Your short-term goal list should include personal goals that impact your professional goals. Many professionals get terribly frustrated because their personal and professional goals seem to clash. The overall reason for this is because they haven't allowed for every short-term goal.

One way to clarify your short-term goals is to make a timetable. Plan it six months out, listing goals for each month. Again, make certain the list contains the personal goals that might impact your job. For example, one guy listed going to the gym three times a week as a short-term goal. With that in mind, he knew he had to think about a job with flextime or one that would get him out of the office by five or six o'clock. A friend who decided to change careers wanted to include her charity work in her daily routine. She made sure to list that on her short term-goal sheet.

It's difficult to separate our personal lives from our professional lives. When many people think about short-term professional goals, they tend to overlook their personal goals. Remember, professional and personal goals affect one another.

As you make your list, keep in mind what makes you smile. If what you'll get from a job—and be realistic—isn't likely to meet your short-term needs or coincide with your personal goals, then you probably won't be happy. Remember, too, that it's short-term goals that motivate us. We all need daily nudges to provide motivation. Without them, we might as well just stay home and watch TV.

ONE SIZE DOESN'T FIT ALL

After taking the tests in the last chapter, you should be on your way to making a job choice that's compatible with your talents and passions. Now that you know *what* you want to do, let's turn our attention to *where* it is you want to work. Your homework assignment in the last chapter was to investigate companies that do the kind of work you're interested in. Now consider whether any of those companies are possible places of employment for you. Perhaps the assignment stimulated some thoughts on what type of company would serve as an appropriate destination.

For example, I talked previously about advertising and choosing a creative position. If that was your choice, consider the options. Do you want to work for an ad agency or the in-house advertising department of a corporation? Maybe you'd like to work for a large printing company that hires full-time creative types for yearly projects such as catalogs. Or you could work for any number of industries that need creative personnel in their advertising departments. The question you'll need to ask yourself: "Which company will best support my occupational choice?" Once you make that determination, you can move on to other particulars, like the terms and conditions of employment you'd accept from the company you've identified.

DOWN THE ROAD: LONG-TERM GOALS

You'll also want to get in touch with your long-term goals. They usually range from a few years hence to many years down the line. Do you want to one day become the president of the company you're working for? Do you hope to acquire enough skills to open your own business in that field? Do you want to start a chain? Do you want to branch out and write a book on your area of expertise? I worked for four years for a public relations firm, which was like an intense four-year university—very hands-on. When I left, I was fully equipped to open my own shop because I knew going in that I would one day want to do that.

What about income? Where do you want to be over the long haul, incrementally and upon retirement? Do you want your job experience to prepare you for another field entirely? If so, what? For example, if you become a graphic designer for an ad agency, do you want to one day become an animator of original characters for Disney? We all have bigger dreams than the one we're living. It's the long-haul mentality that moves all of us forward and gives us hope on tough days.

Make a list of your long-term goals and expectations, and don't forget to include your dreams. These should also include your personal long-term goals, like raising a family. Maybe your personal and professional long-term goals are aligned; maybe they're one and the same. I once vowed I would write and perform my own one-woman sketch and improv comedy show. I did, even though it took me twenty-seven years. The time didn't matter—what mattered was that I achieved my goal. And in the meantime I was directly and indirectly preparing myself for such a feat. Think about your long-term goals and make a year-by-year timetable. What do you hope to achieve at the end of each of your "professional years"? Is your year-by-year plan designed to prepare you for those bigger dreams? Dare to dream big. As my mother used to say, "You have nothing to lose. Dreams are free." Always reaching for something bigger—challenging yourself—is a healthy way to live your professional life.

Dr. Alex Kappas, a renowned southern California psychologist who counsels many celebrities, once told a class of his to write down their dreams, definitively and carefully. He contends that when you take time to transcribe your dreams onto paper, they almost always come true. Dreams in written form penetrate the subconscious, he says.

I once saw comedian/actor Jim Carrey interviewed. He told the story of how, when he was a starving comic, he wrote himself a check for a million dollars, postdated it several years ahead and put it in his wallet. Sure enough, when the date arrived, he'd made that million. For inspiration, make a list of people around you and those throughout history who dared to think long term.

WHO'S THE BOSS?

Another issue to consider when evaluating your personal and professional priorities is whether you want to work for yourself or someone else. There are many advantages to working for a company or corporation, including financial stability (nothing like a regular paycheck), benefit

WORKSHEET: TAKING STOCK OF YOUR PRIORITIES

This itemization will give you a crystal-clear picture of what works and what doesn't relative to your job-related preferences. Consider it your personal checklist for evaluating potential job opportunities when you hear about a job that fits your occupational choice.

1. I've decided I want to be a professional _____
   in the field of _____ .

2. The following is a list of my short-term goals and my timetable, month by month:
   MONTH 1: _____
   MONTH 2: _____
   MONTH 3: _____
   MONTH 4: _____
   MONTH 5: _____
   MONTH 6: _____

3. The following is a list of my long-term goals and my timetable, year by year:
   YEAR 1: _____
   YEAR 2: _____
   YEAR 3: _____
   YEAR 4: _____
   YEAR 5: _____
   YEAR 6: _____

4. I've decided I'd like to work for a: A) Large company or corporation B) Small- to medium-sized business C) Be self-employed.

5. I've decided I want to work within _____ miles of home.

6. I will accept $_____ per year for my services.

7. The following is a list of other terms and conditions I will seek:
   A) _____
   B) _____
   C) _____

8. The following is a list of things I cannot or will not accept at any job (e.g., overtime without pay, an office without a window, an unreasonably demanding boss, etc.):
   A) _____
   B) _____
   C) _____

9. The following is a list of companies within that locale that may provide suitable job opportunities for me (it doesn't matter if I have any connections there; I'll learn to network my way toward what I need):
   A) _____
   B) _____
   C) _____

10. This all sounds great for now, but someday I hope to _____

packages, paid time off, no hassling with self-employment taxes, and chances to move upward or from one department to another. There's also camaraderie, the stimulation of competition, the satisfaction of teamwork, the relief of a helping hand, backup support and company get-togethers.

Having said that, there are also pluses to working for a small business, many of which include the aforementioned. Small businesses also offer other perks such as more control over your immediate environment, input into company policy (a bigger voice) and most importantly, a better chance of moving up. For example, my cousin had little work experience when she divorced and had to return to the workplace. She took a job as an administrative assistant for a company that sells promotional advertising items like pens with the company's name inscribed on them. Over the past six years, she has gone from being an entry-level receptionist to chief executive assistant to the president. The company grew (four employees up to thirty-two), and so did her career. She has been told that she will be asked to serve as president within the next five years.

Then there are two other kinds of work environments: freelancing and being self-employed. As a freelancer you may not have a steady income or constant work flow, but if you're a go-getter you can achieve both your short- and long-term professional and personal goals. I'm more or less a freelancer, and I don't think I could work any other way now. I love my independence and calling my own shots. I can work long hours for one week and take the next week off; I don't have to get permission for such a schedule from my boss—I *am* the boss! Another advantage to freelancing is that you can work out of your home.

Being self-employed is similar to freelancing. However, while many freelancers work alone, one who is self-employed can have many people working for her. The biggest benefits to self-employment are control and the unlimited potential for revenue. The downsides are the overwhelming responsibility of finding and renting your space, marketing your product or service, buying and leasing equipment, payroll and other taxes, licenses, insurance, exposure to lawsuits—the list goes on. But if you're the type who likes to be in charge, enjoys a challenge and is not afraid of risks, then being self-employed should be a strong consideration or a long-term goal. Many of the great American success stories, from Henry Ford to Ted Turner, fall in this category.

In the end, it all relates to how you spelled out your short- and long-term goals. So along with considering where you want to work and what terms and conditions will make you happy, you also need to consider what situation will address your short- and long-term goals. What feels right to you? Is it a large conglomerate? Is it a small- to medium-sized business, or will you be happier going it alone? Make those lists!

COMING TO TERMS

Let's assume you've chosen a profession and a job that meets your short- and long-term goals. Now you'll want to decide where you're willing to work in the geographical sense. Within what mile radius will you be the most comfortable? If driving's not your thing, it makes no sense to take a great job that requires you to be in heavy traffic for hours each day. I once took a terrific job in Los Angeles when I lived in Orange County. After eight months of a one-hour commute, the job didn't seem so terrific anymore. I was so frustrated with the freeway that I was tempted to join the ranks of the road rage set. Make sure your job choice is reasonable in terms of distance.

For some people, commuting is worthwhile if the price is right. While you're thinking about what's worth what, think seriously about what *you're* worth—your salary requirements. Let's say you've decided not to accept less than two thousand dollars a week. Or perhaps you want a full benefit package, bonuses and compensatory time off for an accumulation of long hours. Once you have these conditions in mind, do some research before you set up an interview. It's essential to assess what an employer is likely to offer when setting your priorities. Be realistic about what your current experience is worth, what someone at your skill level might be paid and what unique talents you have that would entice an employer to offer you a higher salary. Like many, do you still have "dues" to pay? What will it take for you to reach the plateau where your goals can be met? Are you willing to take a little less in exchange for a great benefits package, time off, a chance to move up, the opportunity to learn? Maybe you will take a job that pays a little less than what you want, but offers you the chance to advance your skill level so that in six months you can ask for more money. Or it prepares you to make a move that would provide the much-wanted financial increase. Think long-

term first, short-term second, and make certain your short- and long-term goals are realistic and aligned with your needs.

Most of the people I polled about priorities said when they finally hit on the right job choice, their first consideration was where they would work (locale); the second was what the job entailed; the third was what the job would offer in terms of long-term opportunities. Last on their priority list, they said, was money. People often make the mistake of concentrating on the financial aspects of a position instead of considering what would make them happy overall. More importantly, some people don't outline their short- and long-term goals; they simply come upon them by trial and error. So get a great start before you hit the networking trail. Make your list first, and check it twice. You don't want to get enthused about a position that doesn't meet your real priorities and goals.

As you go forward, keep your promises to yourself. Don't waste valuable time networking in circles that won't lead you to that dream job. If you compromise, you may set yourself up for frustration and disappointment. Go back and check your answers. Did you list all your short- and long-term goals? Did you make a timetable? Are your terms and conditions realistic? Can you live with your choices? If you can honestly answer "yes," to each of these, you're ready to move on.

chapter four

Who Do I Know?

As you proceed through this portion of the book, keep in mind that your job right now is to get the job you want. With that as your mind-set, everything you actively do as a result of the following lessons should help you make that happen. Stay focused on that idea. As I mentioned in the introduction, *networking is an activity that enables you to access and link up to appropriate and useful connections to get what you want and need*. In this case, it's a job that you want and need. This part of the book will provide the mechanics and tools to help you *access* useful contacts and *utilize* them effectively.

Later in this section you will get an understanding of the art of networking—how to use your public relations skills and your creative and intuitive processes for networking purposes. You will also learn the fine art of handling people. While the act of networking is extremely important, there is an art side to it as well.

POPPING THE QUESTION— ASKING IT CONSTANTLY

As you search for sources who can help (or hire) you, you'll repeatedly ask: "Who do I know?" If you decide to go after a career in the airline industry, for example, you would ask yourself: "Who do I know that either works in that industry or knows somebody who does?" This is the starting point for any networker, whether you're looking for a source to gain access to some*thing* or some*one*. This applies not only to those just stepping into the workforce, but those who've been in it for any number of years.

EVERYBODY KNOWS SOMEBODY SOMETIME

Your goal in this chapter is to make a long list, beginning with those you know in your industry of choice. They can be friends, relatives or even people you've just met once in passing. You don't have to know the CEO of a large computer company, nor do you have to know someone who has the exact job you're after. Your names can be comprised of individuals remotely connected with the company you're interested in. Let's say you know a guy who works for a company that provides courier service. He frequently has pickups and deliveries at the company you're interested in going to work for. Through his work, he makes small talk with the receptionist. Knowing this, you can tell him you're trying to get your foot in the door so the next time he's at that company, he drops the hint to the receptionist. He asks her who you would contact about a job interview, queries her on what jobs might be open and so on. This delivery guy is a perfect person to put on your list. He doesn't work for the company, but he is remotely connected. That's good enough.

Write down those people you think may know somebody in your field of interest. None of these have to be people you know well, just names that answer the question: "Who do I know that knows somebody in _____ ?"

If you are frustrated, helpless and stymied because you think there's no way to get to the "right" people, the ones that can help you get that job, think about the six-degrees-of-separation theory. That's the concept whereby everybody is connected somehow to somebody else; whoever you want to reach is only six people away from your initial contact. Find people who can steer you to others in your field of interest or people who are already in your desired industry. It's not that hard to "link up" when you put your mind to it. You may only have to go through a half dozen contacts to reach your destination.

Take as much time as you need to compile this list; it will serve as the backbone of your personal resource center. Keep it in a file called "Leads," and add at least six names daily.

CASHING IN YOUR MEMORY BANK

An aspiring actor told me he knew no one in the entertainment industry, though he wanted desperately to work in that field. After asking him to search his memory, Rich recalled an acting coach he had worked with who frequently talked about the fun he had performing as an extra in films. Though this coach was not a heavy hitter in the entertainment industry, he had brushed against it. He certainly knew people who could start a trail for my client. Here's how the progression went: Rich called his former coach Robert (it took him a while to find him, too). Robert put Rich through to his talent agent in Hollywood. The agency recommended two seminars for newcomers in the entertainment industry and a casting director to whom Rich could send his resume. When he sent the resume to the casting director, that person sent Rich on to a commercial acting workshop where he met several other actors, two terrific teachers, and a technical lighting person who worked at Paramount Studios. Rich landed a job in Paramount's preproduction department where he networked with as many co-workers as possible. Through these connections, Rich met a personal manager who agreed to take him on and help guide his acting career. So in his case, Rich got a job in an industry he really liked, affording him a number of opportunities to link up to others who might help him get the job he ultimately wanted: to be a working actor.

I use this example of acting because I think it's one of the harder occupations to break into and one in which it is not always easy to find regular work. If Rich can work from one initial lead to another to get him the Paramount Studios job and an agent, you can get to what you want and need, too.

A highly successful man in his forties contacted me to ask if I knew anyone in the transportation industry—trucking, in particular. He was a salesperson for a company that installed lighting fixtures, but he never really liked his line of work. He said he had a fascination for "how things get from one place to another via ground carriers" and how technology was influencing that field. Since he was a computer whiz, he thought he might be able to bring some innovative changes to a trucking company. He approached me, knowing I wasn't into trucking, but sensing that with my background I might know someone he could call upon. I gave him two names (the editor at a trucking magazine and the brother of a guy who worked for a large California carrier) to start the ball rolling. He was very grateful to me, and I felt good knowing I had helped in some way.

These are just two instances where people contacted direct and indirect sources to utilize networking skills to move them forward in their dream-job pursuit. You can take a good look around and gather up sources that will help move you from one square to the next. We all have contacts that can start a chain reaction; the difficult part is getting off your duff and seeking them out. Unless you live in a cave and have only talked to the animals, you must know someone who can help move you along.

I think the hardest part of this exercise is taking quiet time out to wrack your brain. Think of it as one step at a time. It's like walking along a path of large ceramic stones; just take one at a time. You'll soon discover, with enough effort, contacts you either totally forgot or didn't even think about in this context until you had to. Persistence is the key. Don't slack off in this area; it's the most important beginning to establishing that networking trail.

PLAY THE NAME GAME

Remember that networking is all about relationships, and relationships take people. That's why it's so important for you to play the name game. Here's another way of gathering them: Through the course of our lives, each of us has met people along the way who can help us access others, people who can aim us in the right direction. One way to play the name game is to list different eras in your life—high school, college, early twenties, time in the military service, that semester in grad school, the years you spent as the homeroom parent—and see if you can write down the names of people with whom you had good rapport, even if today you're no longer in touch with them. Doing a little detective work, then picking up the phone and making a call may be one of the smartest investments of your time. If you flashback in your own history, there are a number of people whom you can access, and they just may be able to help you.

A friend of mine who was getting back into the job market after raising three children for fifteen years, felt totally defeated as she put her resume together. She had great credentials, having climbed to the management ranks of a major insurance company. "But that was a long time ago," she bemoaned. "I didn't really stay in touch." So I suggested that she get in touch— that she call the company she last worked for, see who was still on staff who would remember her and see if she could arrange a meeting with them. Even if it's one person, I told her, that's a wonderful start. If none of her co-workers were employed at the old company, I told her to ask around and find out where they had moved to. She did that and found five people who remembered her and her terrific work. Through that small nucleus of people she was able to start a strong networking base. She ultimately got a wonderful position through a contact of a contact of a contact, and it only took her a few weeks to do it. Her success had to do with her ability to capitalize on former relationships—to go back in time and rekindle them.

Your job now is to grab that pencil and paper again and chronicle specific eras in your life. Write down the names of memorable individuals you can look up and see what leads they might provide.

GET CREATIVE

We all have hundreds of contacts if we allow ourselves to take some creative license with the people around us. For example, I spoke to a college graduate who was well educated, had great grades, knew that he wanted to work with children, but swore he knew no one who could help him. He went to school on the East Coast and was looking for a job on the West Coast.

I told him to ask his parents for names of their friends and business associates who might have a business in his area of interest or be connected to someone in that field. When he balked at the idea, confiding that he didn't think his parents could just reel off a roster of names, I told him to ask them to bring their Christmas-card list to the table. He did and was overwhelmed at how many names they provided that proved to be excellent ground-level resources. Through a chain of connections, he landed a job working with children.

Whether you're just out of school, reentering the job market, trying to break into a new industry or trying to further your career in an existing one, you must know someone with names who can get you started. The secret is to get as innovative as you can on where this list might come from. Examples: Your bowling partners, pals who work out at the gym with you, your neigh-

bors, old high school buddies, fellow church members, sorority sisters, fellow support group members, your dentist, your piano teacher, the bank teller, your favorite gift shop owner, your "happy hour" acquaintances, the mechanic who fixes your car . . . Gotcha thinking? Good, keep going!

DROPPING NAMES

While you're making your list of people to contact, don't forget to include names that have the power to open doors. Each of us knows a number of people whose names would make a favorable impression on our prospective employers. I knew a young lady who was looking for a job as a paralegal in a criminal defense law firm. She'd only worked for a firm that handled business litigation, but her uncle was a highly reputed criminal defense attorney in an adjoining city. Just the mere mention of his name during her employment interview got her an opportunity to meet with the final decision maker. She got the job. The logic behind the hirer's decision was that this young lady had been around the "biz" most her life, which was of tremendous value in terms of the learning-curve process.

One of the most valuable assets you can have when approaching your leads is someone's name—the name of the person who referred you to the lead in the first place or someone you know they will perceive to be of value. Using a name each time you introduce yourself on the phone or in your cover letter provides an almost instant door opener. It gets results for two reasons. First, dropping a familiar or respected name creates a sense of comfort and ease at the beginning of any conversation; people are more receptive and the atmosphere is far friendlier. Next, using someone's name provides credibility. Whenever someone calls me whom I *don't* know but uses a name I *do* know, I am much more apt to take the call. I also feel a certain obligation to be of help, especially when it's the child of a friend or business colleague. At times it's hard to get a welcome when you can't drop the name of someone your lead knows and likes. So as you approach potential employers or other networking sources, see if you can have a name to mention.

Ask permission to use your source's name before you meet with any new people that source refers you to. You don't want to tread on your source's generosity. Obtaining the right to drop someone's name is truly a privilege. In the networking process, you'll want to drop names liberally. Careful not to overuse or abuse that right, however. I know people who toss around the names of one or two prestigious contacts as often as their own business cards. Often, they drop them at the most awkward of times. I see this at many of those meet-and-greet business functions. I once watched a guy at an evening association meeting do it so much that when it came to shaking the host's hand, he accidentally introduced himself as the person whose name he had been dropping. His cheeks flushed and he stuttered through his real name while I feigned a coughing spell to camouflage my laughter.

People use an important name to make a favorable impression, but it can do just the opposite if not used properly. My advice: Don't take advantage of using a name. Only drop one if it helps you gain entry or provides a comfort level with the person you're communicating with. In other words, don't flaunt names randomly as you stand around making cocktail chatter at one of those workshops or seminars. Save the mention for times when dropping it can get you some mileage, like during that appointment

with a hot prospect. Sometimes the need to use someone's name too often bespeaks of insecurity. And if the person whose name you're dropping finds out you're leaning on his reputation too much, he may resent it.

It's important that each of us have names to drop within our own industry that will mean something to others. We want to have them at the ready, and we want to use them when it can help us. But be careful to drop a name only once in awhile. Make a list of important people whose names you can drop, and use them only when you need that trump card.

ASSIGNMENTS: NAME THAT NAME

1. Make a list of people who work, or know somebody who works, in the industry you've targeted. If you're already in your industry of choice but wish to advance in some way, ask the same question. Start with your co-workers. Don't overlook friends, neighbors and relatives. Make a special file for this information. Start with no less than one dozen names.

2. Add six names to this list daily.

3. Search your memory for more names. No excuses here. Each of us knows someone in our past who can provide contacts. Make a list of no less than six additional names to add to your networking database.

4. If you are a first-time networker, make up a list creatively. Earlier we talked about the young man who culled names from his parents' Christmas-card list as a starting point. Now it's your turn to do something similar. Even if you have other names, find an innovative way to make yet another list; it will either augment or bolster what you already have. Get at least twenty names. The trick is to go to one source who may have a long list of excellent contacts,

all of whom could provide assistance (or a job). Now work those leads for even more names. Record these along with what you've gathered so far.

5. Go back in time and separate your life into important eras. Make a list of those people whom you most remember and who would most remember you. Start your detective work and get their phone numbers or addresses. Now contact them, and see what leads they can provide.

I'll let you off easy on this one: two eras and six names. The rule in this assignment is that you must make contact with each of the six. If not, keep digging until you reach the goal.

6. Through the course of your search, see what people you can handpick from your list that would be terrific names to drop. Get their permission to refer to them. The field is wide open on this one, but no fair getting less than one.

You just collected no less than fifty-six leads. Congratulations! You now have dozens of names to start your network base. Don't forget, you were asked to add at least six names each day. After four weeks you'll have 168 additional sources. Yes, it takes diligence, but remember the perseverance principle. Don't forget to set up an excellent filing system or database, because when you start getting up there in numbers, you'll need a way to stay organized. For now, take it day by day. Stay consistent and honor your goals.

chapter five

Where Do I Go?

In addition to making contact with individuals, there are other ways to get to where you want to go. They require conscientiousness in your search for information and doggedness in your pursuit of accessible resources. There isn't any job in the world that doesn't have an available pool of resources around it; all you have to do is find them. One of the first ways to begin exploring your resources requires using your intuition and instincts to create possibilities.

USE YOUR IMAGINATION AND INTUITION

Networking means connecting with people you don't know yet. How successful you'll be at networking largely depends on how you use your imagination and intuition. You've got to tap into your creative self and explore what you find there.

First let's examine your inner resources. They are abundant; you simply need to take advantage of them. Those of you with metaphysical roots know that when you're struggling with a problem, a quiet, meditative moment often helps you find the perfect solution. Sit still, close your eyes and take a deep breath. It is a wonderful way to tap into a place where ideas and possibilities come at you like tennis balls out of an automated machine. Each of us has a ready, ample supply of this kind of intuition, but we don't often use it. Looking within for insight is a great way to start the groundwork for networking.

The first step in the networking process—going from nowhere to somewhere and nothing to something—is to gather ideas. Consider the basis of networking a mental thing initially. Later it becomes a more physical or active process.

Your mental garden is a fertile starting point that can get you moving toward the contacts you need to get that job you want. When you open up your mind, you go beyond the obvious.

RUNNING ON EMPTY

My daughter, who had been a successful buyer in the fashion industry for several years, knew she wanted out of that hectic business, but didn't know where to direct her talents. After making her "positive identification," she declared that the field of interior design would be a great lateral move. After all, if she could outfit a person, she could outfit a sofa.

"Where to start, though," she said to me one day.

I instructed her to take an afternoon away from everything, grab a pencil and paper and just sit and relax. I told her to let her mind wander and let her thoughts lead her. I told her to jot down every possibility that bounced off her mental trampoline, no matter how random it seemed, including ideas as to how she might break into the interior design business. I told her to ask herself where she could go for guidance and contacts but not to worry about whether or not she could produce answers.

After about an hour she had written down the following ideas, all of which proved to be viable places to contact: interior design studios, her friend's mother (who decorated model homes), the art and home economic departments of local colleges and universities, the library (for names of publications that catered to the interior design industry), the Internet, furniture stores, local home builders and the phone book.

They were all decent choices, although she later told me that the phone book turned out to be one of the most plentiful resources. Not only was there a long list of interior design firms, there were also related headings—"Flooring," "Carpeting" and "Window Coverings"—that created a slew of leads. When she called all those listed under "related categories," they led to a host of referrals to interior designers.

You can originate sources from nowhere and get to somewhere in a hurry. It doesn't take a lot of time and effort, either. Just a quiet afternoon, a pencil and a piece of paper. When you take a time out—a meditative moment—you get a flood of ideas via your own intuition. And don't overlook those weird moments when, out of nowhere, you suddenly get a hunch. Record those, too. Ideas are abundant, but we need an open mind to usher them in.

Always remember: When it comes to networking, one lead leads to another, whether it's ideas or contacts.

CLIMB EVERY MOUNTAIN

Another part of your ability to network has to do with your sense of adventure, your ability to be imaginative and carefree as you check out your leads. A mountain climber will tell you to get to a higher plateau you must be willing to explore and take chances.

My daughter pursued her initial leads spontaneously, wide-eyed and open-minded, taking in all the "sights" along the way. She promised herself she would travel great lengths to reach her final destination, treating each journey with a purpose and a sense of positive anticipation and expectancy. "You never know what you'll run into," she later told a friend. "It's fun to just explore every possibility."

Granted, she ran into some roadblocks and detours along the way, but more often than not, she accumulated contacts, made valuable friends and learned a great deal.

You can enjoy the same sense of discovery as you explore your initial ideas. Let your intuition lead the way. View each exploration like a visual artist would a canvas; it's completely blank but can be filled with wonderful images. In your case, those images are ideas of where you might go for job possibilities. So paint vividly! Or, if this picture resonates more with you, think of yourself as an investigative reporter going for a story or a detective solving a crime. Both will tell you their work is full of adventure as they dig for answers.

As you explore, give yourself permission to step off track. If one destination suddenly suggests another, investigate. Think of all the discoveries the world would have missed if scientists, explorers and astronauts had one-track minds. Ask yourself this question: What interesting destination did you recently discover that could lead to another?

The lesson here: Meditate, listen and explore.

TAPPING INTO CONCRETE SOURCES

Any businessperson's knack for research is a strong asset, whatever your job or field, and one that is essential if you want to advance throughout your career. You can't network very far without a penchant for seeking out information that will guide you. This part of your journey is where you'll focus on the scientific side of networking as well as the more creative aspects. Coming upon contacts takes analysis, time and diligence.

We've covered the how-to of meeting people on an individual basis, so let's discuss the how-to of expanding your overall networking base. You can do this by locating groups, organizations, associations, institutions and the media. These resources can open up additional networking opportunities that put you smack-dab in the middle of where you need to be to meet individuals who can help or hire you. Good digging skills—skills that allow you to expand and broaden your horizons and use what you find to your advantage—are vital.

GETTING YOUR STUFF TOGETHER

Think of this part of your quest as setting up and organizing an extensive database, because that's what you'll be doing. To network well you have to be extremely organized. Your sense of order will pay off over time because you'll be adding to your concrete resources continually. In effect, you'll be creating your very own resource center, your library. You will often resort and add to this center for the rest of your professional career. There are a number of computer programs, such as ACT! and Claris FileMaker Pro, that assist with this. If you don't have a PC, you can still make file folders to contain all your information. This exercise is similar to our earlier exercise in which we explored your potential and sought out job opportunities that matched your capabilities. You can simply add what you collect now to the filing system you started then.

Each time you come upon an organization or association that is of interest or could help you, make sure you record the pertinent information about it in the appropriate file. For example, if you're looking for different events that may be integral to your career pursuits, make a file for chambers of commerce within your geographical region. Chambers always sponsor great events. There are other basic categories to create in your reference center as well. Your database should not have so many categories that you confuse yourself and have your information scattered about, but just enough broad headings to keep your sources organized. In addition to a Chambers of Commerce file, you might also want:

- Workshops and Seminars
- Trade Organizations and Associations
- Clubs and Groups
- Libraries and Institutions
- Books of Lists
- Media—Print and Electronic
- The Internet
- Books and Reference Materials

WORKSHOPS AND SEMINARS

No matter what profession you're in, you always have something more to learn. Where you choose to go to learn will always be a great addition to your database. As an improvisational comedy teacher and director, I take at least one class every six months to add to my repertoire of skills. If you want to move up the corporate ladder to a bigger and better position, apply your current skills to a different field or build a knowledge base from scratch; there is nothing more valuable than lectures, classes, workshops and seminars that address your craft or passionate job desire. This is especially important if you want to change jobs. I have a friend who worked as a cameraman for a local ABC affiliate. He liked the field but wanted to get into the editing part of the business, so he spent two years taking every class and workshop possible to prepare for that move. In the process, he made a lot of valuable contacts, and so can you—folks who may know about openings and opportunities or who would be willing to share their networking contacts with you. Today my friend is a major motion picture film editor.

Your next assignment is to identify all the educational opportunities out there. Some resources that might help you are:

- newspaper and magazine calendar listings
- the Internet
- your local chamber of commerce
- your favorite industry organization
- your friends
- college extension courses and community college offerings
- educational and vocational centers, including the YWCA and the YMCA

Find out what study opportunities are available that could provide you with more informa-tion and skill. Making study a staple in your initial networking effort is an excellent way to begin the start-up of that database center.

SAVE ALL YOUR MAILERS

If you're already in the industry you want to be in and just don't have the position you've dreamed of, save all your mailers (most of us refer to it as junk mail). They provide a catalog of what's being offered in the way of study relevant to you. Each day I get at least three to four pieces of junk mail promoting classes and workshops, all of which would put me in contact with people I want and need to know. Often the advertised events focus on something new or "cutting edge," so they can be a good way to stay current in your targeted field.

Assemble a decent file of study opportunities, and sign up for something at least once a month, including:

- lectures
- seminars
- workshops
- college courses (extension, community college or otherwise)
- industry association and organization educational events
- trade shows
- symposiums (such as career development)

To find out which workshops and seminars are adequately priced and worthwhile, call the number on the mailer and ask for referrals or call others who have taken such classes and get their feedback. Always ask for several independent referrals and a good cross section of testimonials. Many organizations have "shills" (people whom the organization has made arrangements with to give a thumbs up to those who call—more commonly known as "plants"), but what you're after is honest input, not a biased opinion. See how long the organization sponsoring the class or workshop has been around and how many people have gone through its courses. Also, check who has endorsed the organization's work and what their credentials are. If someone has worked with Fortune 500 companies or with those I know in my industry, I know they're probably viable sources for courses.

If you're uncertain about price or fees, call competitors and ask what they're charging for similar classes. You can sometimes take the same course through a community college that is offering it independently at an outside facility, and the course is either free or available for just a registration fee. Don't take all the hype on the flier as truth. Investigate. There are so many wonderful classes and workshops available. Just make certain what you've enrolled in is reputable and worth your time.

Save your mailers in a file labeled "Mailers"; it may serve as a great resource down the line. You may not have time or money to take a class today, but a year from now, you might.

This literature is more valuable than you think. For one thing, it almost always lets you know what is current in your industry of interest. The most recent ideas are usually introduced in some type of flier as an enticement to get you to attend an event that offers something new. At least one-third of the business-oriented junk mail I receive is for some workshop or seminar that boasts a new and revolutionary way to network.

So before you toss that "junk mail," look it over. Maybe there's something of value to you.

TRADE ORGANIZATIONS AND ASSOCIATIONS

Look into what is available in your industry. There is normally a wide selection of organiza-

tions that bring people together for no other reason than knowledge and networking.

Whatever your field of interest, chances are good that you will find trade organizations and associations dedicated to serving and supporting people in your field. These groups exist to help members acquire new information about their field and offer them educational opportunities, support systems, forums for sharing information and a host of other resources. The Direct Mail Marketing Association, for instance, has local chapters to help members. It also offers conferences, yearly conventions, printed materials with the latest and greatest technology and counseling services, among other things. Similar organizations in your field can help you with your goals and objectives.

As you add these sources to your database, make sure they are sources that count. Don't clutter your files with meaningless groups and organizations with which you have nothing in common. There are many excellent national organizations, but you want to join associations where you can be active and derive substantial benefits. This means adding groups to your list that are easy to access. Here are some guidelines:

- Are you within realistic driving distance to their events?
- Do they meet often enough to do you good?
- Do they have a good reputation? What meaningful and credible references can they provide?
- Are you likely to make networking contacts? Ask some of their existing members if their affiliation created valuable contacts and in what way.
- Can they add to your career goals? Does joining a particular group create a career advancement opportunity either through contacts or education?

- Does your affiliation help market you to the business community?

Be somewhat selective; you can't get involved in everything. Delineate on your database which groups you will keep for reference and which will be helpful to join, and of course, which are prime for you to become actively involved in.

A friend of mine was an interior designer who wanted to work with home builders; she had tired of doing home remodels for other individuals. She joined the Building Industry Association's Sales and Marketing Council where she socialized with marketing directors in the real estate industry, as well as builders and developers. After picking up one account, she promptly got another. Within a few years of schmoozing she had cornered the market. She's now an award-winning model home decorator and one of the most successful in the real estate industry.

Your assignment: Join at least three organizations or associations where you can attend the functions they offer. Stacy Sacco, a marketing executive who has served as president of the American Marketing Association, says don't just join to join. Choose at least one organization with the understanding that you will commit to become actively involved—on a committee, for example, doing volunteer work that gets you known and appreciated. Taking a leadership role in any group, says Sacco, can be one of the best career moves you can make. "It creates a positive impression, and that impression will follow you for years," he says.

CLUBS AND GROUPS

In addition to industry-related organizations and associations, you can join a number of clubs and groups to further your database and contacts. This might include anything from your local health or yacht club to Mensa, a national organization whose members tout genius IQs (I am not a member, I only know people who are). I have one friend, an environmentalist, who joined the Sierra Club; another hangs out with a group called The Single Gourmet, where members go to interesting and pricey restaurants together. They both have a blast networking along the way. One of the best affiliations for a business colleague of mine: The Mighty Ducks Hockey Team Booster Club. He changed jobs because of a networking contact he met through them, and he also met his wife as a result of his membership.

What's in your community? Get social.

When I mention this to those I counsel about networking, they all say they never thought about social events as a means to network if the event didn't have something to do with their specific business activities. For some reason, most people spend a great deal of their time seeking out only industry-related societies.

If you don't already belong to a social club or group, join one that isn't too time-consuming. Find a group that will provide stimulation, interest and fellowship, along with the possibility of creating networking opportunities.

I have one friend, a marriage and family counselor, who belongs to seventeen different clubs, though she's not terribly active. She can't possibly attend all their meetings, but she still is listed on their membership rosters. She says the most valuable part of her affiliation is reading their regular newsletters. Her criteria for joining a club are that she have some deep personal interest in the group, that they send out regular reading materials, that they do something to help others and that she be allowed copies of each club's membership roster. The names on these rosters are in her database under "Club Members." She sends out a quarterly newsletter on her work—findings and topics of interest to families—to each of these people. She claims her list numbers 2,030, and she's received 40 percent of her referral business as a result of her mailings. Granted, her membership fees are hefty, but she feels it's worth it. Get busy and creative; join a club or two.

LIBRARIES AND INSTITUTIONS

Another great method of adding to your resource center is to look up various institutions and dump them to your database. Public libraries within a five-mile radius should be listed on your resource sheet, for example. There are hundreds of institutions throughout the country that provide resource materials and information that could help you, whether you're after contacts or job information. For example, if you're trying to find all the associations in the country that offer membership to people in the computer programming industry, the library is a great way to retrieve such information. The library is also a great place to gather information on one or many leaders in your industry. If you want to research a magazine piece from two years back that featured a series on unusual entrepreneurs, the library is even better than the office of the publication itself. Virtually any networking list can be found at a library. Not only does this public institution provide materials, there is also always someone there to help you.

Another wonderful library resource is *Books in Print*, which lists every book currently in print by title, author, subject or publisher. You can also look up publications (purchase copies, too) in select editions of Bacon's *Publicity Checker* or Amalia Gebbie's *All-In-One Directory*. These two

resources list all the newspapers, magazines and radio and television stations in the country. Bacon's also publishes a special book for international media contacts. Their reference books are invaluable. They list the publications, describe their demographics, name every editor in each department and provide addresses and phone numbers. *The Reader's Guide to Periodical Literature* is yet another great source for finding the information you need.

There are other private and public institutions that you can access for information on any subject. I once spent two whole days browsing through the Library of Congress in Washington, D.C.; their resources are overwhelming. There is an institution for every field, and the library is a great first source for finding who and where these institutions are.

Many professions have unions. For example, the Musicians Union is a great way to access instructors, musicians, historical music information and rare musical instruments. These unions can tell you what is hot in their industry and keep you up on the latest news. Whatever union affects your work should be listed on your database under "Institutions." What other institutions should be included on that list? Colleges? Training centers? Museums? The latter may amuse you, but think how much information the Smithsonian Institutions have at the ready. I've written to them on many occasions for demographics and statistics that I couldn't have found anywhere else.

There are at least a few institutions that you'll want to have handy as you network. List at least five that fit your needs.

BOOKS OF LISTS

Carol Cranfield, the human resource specialist I spoke about earlier, says one of the best resources is a "Book of Lists," which you can find by contacting your local business journal. Most major cities have business publications that issue yearly books of local businesses with their areas of specialty and how to reach the contact persons. Libraries often keep these in their reference departments. These books often include the names of CEOs, company presidents and major consultants. Not only can you find individuals, you also can find names of companies, large and small, that fit your scope of interest.

Add to your database every company that interests you, along with names of the senior management team members or owners. Cranfield tells her charges to contact these sources directly for interviews or referral contacts. Her recommendation: Go for lunch, if possible.

I currently have a list of every human resource manager of every Fortune 500 company across the country (most hire trainers like me). I update and add to it constantly. It's a lifeline for a management consultant like me, who relies almost exclusively on interest from human resource departments, for they usually hire all training specialists.

Let's say you make a trip to the library. What books of lists would suit your database? Make photocopies, or if the list is too long, write down the name of the book and order a copy from the publisher. If you can't fit all the names in your database, you can fit that book on your shelf. Store it there for easy reference. Each of us should have a small library of books that we refer to (which I'll cover a little later in this chapter). You can also contact the International Research Council; they have a collection of books on just about anything.

Make sure your database includes prominent, key people you want to get to know, whether for networking reasons or getting hired.

PRINT AND ELECTRONIC MEDIA

One of the quickest ways to gain insight and knowledge about your field and/or passion is through the media. Because access is so widespread, media outlets are probably our finest resource, whatever it is we're trying to find. Whether the media is print or electronic, there are up-to-the-minute reports every day that address all industries. As business professionals, each of us must check in with the media, either morning or evening, to find out the latest news.

One of the things I most like about using the media as a resource is that most news programs have a research department; no matter what you're looking for, they've got something on it. Most research assistants are good about taking a call from an outsider and either giving them the information they need or referring them on. If, for instance, you're looking for a club that offers membership to forensic accountants, they'll either tell you the name of one or tell you where you can find one. Their worlds move so fast, and they are required to be so knowledgeable, it's hard to challenge them by asking for a source they don't know about.

I don't recommend calling your local radio or news station, nor do I advocate calling the desk of your local newspaper every time you need something. But I do recommend doing the following every day:

• Read a consumer newspaper or magazine, such as *Time* and *Newsweek*, that offers reports on all that is going on in the world. There are many others I strongly suggest you subscribe to. Almost every single successful business executive reads voraciously. There are both national and weekly magazines; at least one of them will be of help and interest to you.

• Thoroughly peruse a trade or business journal directly affiliated with your field of expertise or interest. This may be your most important task, as you use the media for insight and info. What's happening in your corner of the business community is critical to your own career growth. Make sure you're up on the latest trends and news.

• Daily or weekly newspapers are also a must. I know some business people who read *The Wall Street Journal* religiously. Any one of the major national daily newspapers is a must, such as the *Los Angeles Times*, *The New York Times*, *The Washington Post* and the *San Francisco Chronicle*.

There are actually two hundred major newspapers across the country. Read your local paper and one that provides national and international news. One of my personal favorites is *USA Today*.

• Watch at least one television program—network, cable or local—that is covering something in or related to your field. News magazine-type shows like *Dateline*, *20/20* and *PrimeTime Live* and talk shows such as *Oprah* are informative. There are also specials every week. Almost every cable network in every region of the country offers business news broadcasts, too.

• If you have the capability, go online every day to see what's happening on the Internet, the most thorough resource center we have available today.

• Clip articles of interest and videotape shows you may want to review later. Keep these in appropriate files. You never know when you may need them as you maneuver your way along the resource path.

Here's a fun homework assignment: Make a list of people you've read about, seen or heard, and write or call them. Contact at least two people per week. This is just one more way to schmooze and learn.

I have one friend, an attorney, who has a dozen media contacts in the legal media that she stays in touch with regularly. She's built up some solid relationships over the years, and all have been helpful to her when she can't access information any other way. She makes herself available to them as well, as an expert source for their questions in the field of family law. If you have something to offer the media, they are always glad to hear from you. If not, feel free to plug into them for help; they're pretty good about giving you time and resources. Too, this is another great way to establish networking relationships as you research. Think about contacting a media source directly, one that you can stay in touch with on a regular basis. You can also contact the media to reach a person who has been interviewed or profiled on their show.

THE INTERNET

The "net" in Internet says it all. Networking via the Internet is clearly the wave of the future and probably the fastest way to get information we want and need. I know people who don't use any other source for their research.

It's easy to look things up on the Internet, and you can talk to others, asking questions and getting answers via E-mail or through instant messages (chatting back and forth).

Although advances in technology allow us to quickly and easily gain access to information, they also lure us into bypassing the traditional reference books by getting answers, "saving" them and logging off. Before I log off, though, I print out a hard copy and file it for added insurance.

Plugging into the Internet has other advantages: You can get up-to-the-minute news instantly and access various organizations, associations, clubs, groups and institutions.

The good news gets even better. More Web pages are added every single month; the technology and resources multiply at a phenomenal rate. Costs for such technology are becoming far more reasonable, and we can expect nothing less in the future. If you don't have a PC or an account with an Internet service provider, you can use a computer at a library or school. There are also several places that rent computers linked to the Internet. I know of a young lady who doesn't have the means for a computer yet, but she rents time every week to meet her needs. There are no excuses for not getting acquainted with and using the Internet. I first hated computers and the complications online access posed; now I have no idea how I functioned without them.

One mistake many people make when using the Internet is that they don't transfer the information they've located to their personal database. Immediately transfer the information you have gathered onto your PC, or print it out and put it in your hard-copy files. You still can't get some things from the Internet, like the contents of a good trade book, which is why you need all the above resource centers to retreat to. Besides, it's not a good idea to have only one place to go for information. What happens if your computer crashes or your online service happens to go off line when you suddenly need something right away? You always want to have several options for getting what you need.

BOOKSTORES

Though today we have many ways to access and gather information, nothing is more valuable than a good book on the subjects that interest you. We're in the age of self-help heaven, where there is a how-to manual on just about everything. (I saw a book recently on how to buy a sweater for your dog!) Taking a leisurely afternoon to browse at a well-stocked bookstore is a calming and energizing experience that can saturate you with ideas, facts, sources and contacts. Spending unlimited time in a bookstore is like a religious experience to me. When I'm done there, I have a sense of fulfillment like that of going to church. I feel somehow richer and more complete, and I usually have four or five books that I can't wait to get home and read.

Bookstores are also great resources to find reference books and unique magazines and periodicals. I've come upon magazines I didn't even know existed by browsing through a bookstore's magazines racks. I found a magazine called *AutoTrader*, which allows people to advertise their cars or network with other car enthusiasts for dealing, trading or finding vintage automobiles. If there's an industry, there's a publication for it.

ASSIGNMENTS: WHERE DO I GO?

The lessons in this chapter are integral to your success as a networker, so don't slide on any of the following assignments.

1. Generate a list of sources for potential contacts. Take time out and sit quietly. Let your mind go as you gather ideas. Before you move on to any other activity, write your entire list down.

2. Find out what classes, seminars and workshops are available, and sign up for one. Take at least one every six months. Continue to study your areas of interest whether you're in the job you really want or you're trying to get it. Seeking out classes and workshops throughout your career is a great habit to get into no matter what stage your career is in.

3. Join at least three industry-related organizations or associations. Attend their functions as often as you can, and get actively involved in at least one of them. Make friends and market yourself.

4. Join a club or group that is not necessarily career related but will provide networking opportunities. As I mentioned, my friend joined seventeen clubs and garnered great leads from her affiliations.

5. Visit an institution or two, and see what information and resources are available to assist you in your career goals. Starting with a library card is a wonderful beginning. Research the institutions that may be beneficial to your career endeavors. Keep a list of at least five in your database with notations on what they have to offer and for what purpose you may contact them.

6. Every industry has books of lists that include names, addresses and phone numbers of companies, management team members and others who are direct sources for your needs. Go to the library and research what lists would fit your needs. Include entries from such lists in your database.

7. Don't forget your media assignments. Read a consumer newspaper or magazine daily, especially local ones. Read a trade or business journal regularly. Watch a network or cable television program that addresses your industry or career interest, and record your findings. Either tape these shows for later reference or take notes; clip and tape are the bywords, here. Take a chance and write to some of the people you read or see as a result of your media watch. You may be astounded at the responses you receive and what you'll learn. Your favorite media outlets should also be included in your database files.

8. If you can, check the Internet to gain more resources. Surfing the Web is a fun research

adventure and the wave of the future. The Internet may well be your most visited resource center. If you don't have a PC and can't get online, network until you find someone who will share. Gather pertinent information through this source.

9. Get that personal library going. Begin collecting reference books and materials that will aid you in your networking activities and dream-job search. Even though technology provides us with a great deal of easy-to-access information, there is still nothing more valuable than a library of books that relates to your career needs and goals.

KEEP YOUR RECORDS STRAIGHT

As you accumulate your resources, however you choose to do it, make certain you keep easy-to-understand, retrievable records.

Make notes next to associations and clubs, describing what they do and how they can help you. Write down reminders next to media contacts. Note short descriptions of institutions and why they exist. Jot down those books you want to add to your personal library. Get familiar with the Internet and all it has to offer as a research tool.

Add frequently to your database; it will soon become your most valuable asset as you move forward and continue to network. You'll come to rely on this as the cornerstone of all your contact making.

Spend as much time as it takes to conduct thorough research. Investigate every lead, and set up a variety of places to go when you need specific information. Our research, and the resources we connect to, determines the success we'll experience in our respective careers. Without a substantial database, you'll find yourself starting from scratch each time you want to make a change in your career.

Your personal library and your personal resource center are the two most important things to fall back on throughout your career, whether you're networking or job searching.

Your reference files are the tangible results of all that research and networking. They're what you have to show for the energy you've expended. I can't stress keeping orderly records and frequently updating your reservoir enough. The information you collect will impact everything you do as you network your way through your professional life.

Every successful executive I interviewed had a database of names, addresses and phone numbers of people and organizations, along with lists, reference materials and bibliographies to aid them. Each of them told me their database was their ultimate treasure, something they would use at different times for different reasons throughout their professional careers.

Whether you're entering the job market, reentering it or have been in it for a long time, an organized file of contacts that you can refer to at will is an absolute must.

chapter six

Making Contacts

OK, you've got your list of people, organizations and groups to contact: Now it's time to approach them. As you act upon the leads you've listed, you will have days when you feel exhausted and defeated; everybody does. But you can't give up—those days are just part of the game. I told you in the introduction that productive and successful networking takes three things: determination, creativity and perseverance. I want you to scribble these down in places you view frequently, like your briefcase, day planner, car dashboard, bathroom mirror, desktop—wherever you tend to look throughout the day.

Before you make that first phone call or send that first package, fix your mind in a state of resolve: No matter how many walls you run into, you won't abandon your crusade until you land the job you want.

Along with your "creativity, determination and perseverance" mantra, write down a menu of affirmations to keep you on course. Also, post these in places where you know your eyes will

land frequently, and say them to yourself throughout each day, especially when you're having a tough moment. Also recite them each night as you fall off to sleep. Your subconscious will grab on to those thoughts and make them materialize. One of my favorites is: "I think I can, I think I can. I thought I could!"

In a book about his life as a developer, Donald Trump listed perseverance as the single most important reason for his success. His attitude is if you keep "plugging away," something great will happen. And he's right.

HELLO THERE

To make contact with your contacts from the list you've carefully gathered, start either of two ways: You can make an initial phone call, or you can send them your background information in the mail (or via E-mail).

THE PHONE

Let's say you go the phone call route. Your goal during the call is to get a personal meeting with this contact or to have them forward you on to others. Let the person know you won't take more than fifteen minutes of her time. Clearly explain what you need: You want to know if she will steer you in the direction of people or businesses who might hire you. Let her know how much you appreciate the time she's taking out of her busy day. Be thankful and gracious, but never patronizing. If she says she doesn't have the time to meet with you, ask if she would be willing to review your package. Most people will say "yes." If it's a "no," don't worry—better not to waste your time and materials, anyway.

I always think the phone call method is better to start your networking because you make that human connection right away, and you get the chance to "make friends." By the time you meet in person, you've already established the beginnings of a relationship—you're halfway there. If the person doesn't want to meet but is willing to give you leads on the phone, be prepared to take notes.

We will thoroughly cover your public relations and communication techniques in subsequent chapters, but I want to mention that your skills in this area take tremendous grace, agility, diplomacy and sensitivity. To make the human connection we so badly need to build our networking base is truly an art unto itself.

Every telephone conversation, short or long, should be well done on your part. Think of good communication as an art form, with yourself as an impresario.

Because communication training is the bulk of my every day work, I pay more attention to conversations than most people do. But for networkers, paying close attention is a must. When the point of conversation is to get people to help you, you can't afford to make mistakes. Consider the following conversation in which

Sam is trying to locate a wedding-cake maker for whom he hopes to work:

SAM: Hi! Hey, is this the printer that knows the cake lady?

PRINTER: Huh? What?

SAM: You know the wedding cake lady? The one that makes the couples that look like real couples? See, I'm a sculptor—

PRINTER: Who is this?

SAM: You're probably busy, so just give me her number?

PRINTER: (Click. Dial tone.)

Sam's dialogue in this hypothetical conversation is obviously inappropriate, but I hear things like this all the time. To begin with, Sam wasn't clear with his reason for calling. His tone was also a bit self-centered and abrupt. Let's see what happens when he listens to the person who answers the phone and the result he gets when he is more specific with his reason for calling:

SAM: Hi! This is Sam. I'm a friend of your receptionist, Sara. Hope I didn't get you at a bad time.

PRINTER: Well, I'm kind of busy, but . . .

SAM: I'm sorry, I didn't catch your name.

PRINTER: Peter.

SAM: Oh, nice to meet you, Peter.

PRINTER: Thanks.

SAM: Sure. Hey, Sara said you had the name and phone number of a lady who makes wedding cakes that feature original designs of the married couple. I'm a sculptor, and I'm trying to reach her to inquire about a job. Would you mind giving me her information, if it's handy?

PRINTER: Oh, yeah. That's Mandy Wilson. She's in Austin. Her number is (555) 567-3429.

SAM: Hey, thanks. Really appreciate it.

PRINTER: No problem. Have a nice day.
SAM: I will now, thanks to you!
PRINTER: Hey great! Bye.
SAM: Bye, now.

As you can see, Sam has a more personal, professional and courteous tone in the second conversation. His attitude is more respectful. He clearly provides information about what he wants and needs, and knowing the printer is busy, he wisely makes his request quickly and politely. If he has to call again, chances are the printer will remember him favorably.

Pay more attention to what you say to others. More importantly, look at your ability to converse with others as an art, because it really is. As you build contacts, interview with potential bosses and establish yourself in the business world, you'll want to master the art of "talk." To mess up in this area could be costly.

LISTEN UP

When you meet with a potential networking connection, either in person or on the phone, don't forget to use your ears. State your questions or request, then listen. Don't make the mistake of listening only until you get what you want. I have seen a number of wanna-be business professionals who bulldoze their way into someone's business life and flatten any kind of goodwill by cutting them off midsentence. They only listen until they get what they want. Fact is, the person trying to help you may have more they want to say. Be attentive, courteous, appreciative and thankful. Those should be your objectives when meeting and conversing with any networking contact.

Never brush aside or deride an idea or suggestion from a potential contact. Whether or not you think their recommendations are worth-

while, show some diplomacy. Remember, they are offering their time to help you; they certainly think what they're telling you is important, so nod politely and go with the flow. You can always discard information later, but don't be rude or ungrateful in anyone's presence.

I once sat in a meeting with a young banker who was looking for some leads from a mortgage broker friend of mine. When my friend told the banker he should attend a seminar on "Making Loans—Making Friends," he started laughing. He said, "I've got friends, I know how to write loans, I need a job and I'm here to see if you're hiring. I can't believe you would suggest I do that." My mouth dropped. So did the banker's name—right off my friend's list. What an inappropriate response. Most of us have our own opinions and approaches, but when we're reaching out to contacts for recommendations and leads, we want to be diplomatic. You can't afford to offend anyone in the business world, so be gracious under any and all circumstances. Today's flunky may be tomorrow's boss.

MAIL CALL

Let's say you skip the phone call and send your packages out to the names you compiled. Make sure you have at least six packages ready to go at all times (you never know when you'll need them). They should include a cover letter, resume and sample of your work. Follow up with a phone call no sooner than four days and no later than ten days after you send the packages. When you call, remember your good manners, your upbeat persona and your clear message. Your job at that point is to get an appointment with the person you've sent your materials—to get him to *want* to meet you in person. When you get there, you can sell yourself. Hopefully, he will either hire you (if he's the appropriate source for that) or help with contacts that move you to the next square.

VOICE MAIL

This type of phone conversation can be your friend or foe. Voice mail is great because you get the perfect opportunity to leave a precise message. The receiver can hear the upbeat tone in your voice, you can explicitly explain your reason for calling and you know the specifics you're leaving will be heard exactly as you said them. In other words, no one mixes up your message, as can happen by a busy secretary who chooses only the details *she* feels are important.

Voice mail affords us the opportunity to have a partial conversation—we can speak our mind. When the person returns our phone call, she can get right to the point without you explaining your reason for calling all over again.

Now the downside: Voice mail records your message exactly as you say it. With most systems you get only one chance to do that. You can't erase your message and start again (although some systems ask if you want to record again). How you sound and what you say is what the receiver will hear when he retrieves his messages. It's important then that you have no regrets. Don't leave a message you wish you could take back. Rehearse any important voice mail message before leaving it. I caution you, though, don't get too rehearsed; it will sound like you're reading lines from a play. You want your message to sound spontaneous and confident.

Whatever message you leave, don't ramble. No one wants to listen to a lengthy discourse; they have other messages to get to and other things to do. Keep your messages short, simple and easy to understand. Nothing is worse than being unable to decipher what someone is saying or having to listen to someone drone. Be especially careful when leaving your phone number; say it slowly and clearly. Many people reel off a number so fast, the message retriever has to play it back several times to get the number right.

E-MAIL

Communicating by E-mail is also a viable way to contact individuals. On the positive side, your messages can be short, sweet and to the point, saving everyone time; on the negative side, they can seem curt and distant. You also run the risk of being too formal or too informal.

The rule here is to send E-mail as you would leave a telephone message. Keep it friendly but to the point, succinct and easy to assimilate.

It may not be appropriate to leave an E-mail message, depending on who you're reaching out to. You need to know their business culture before making that decision.

The following is a suggestion for an E-mail message that falls somewhere in between not too formal and somewhat friendly:

To: XYZ Stationers
Re: Job Openings

Dear Mr. Schwartz:

Learned from a colleague you might be interviewing for sales personnel soon. I am certainly qualified to join your company. Shall I send resume?
Thanks for your reply,

Sandy Betner

CONTACT NAME	COMPANY	PHONE	DATE CONTACTED—
Peter Brown	Bronson Inc.	(555) 375-9872	11/3/99

FOLLOW-UP DATE—
11/8/99

COMMENTS/NOTES
Nice guy but rushed. Said may want to meet first week in December.

LEADS:
Said call Don Miller—Brigdon Corp. (555) 467-2398
Has openings for administrative assistants.

This is brief and concise and precludes Mr. Schwartz from having to read through a lengthy message to get the point. Always keep your E-mail tight. "Think in sound bites," a friend told me recently about composing E-mail. He said that's how people want to communicate electronically. I receive E-mails every day, and I agree that the shorter ones are more easy to quickly assimilate. I don't have time to pour through several paragraphs of copy to get to the heart of any message. E-mail was designed to move information faster and more efficiently, so what we send via it should comply.

MAKING A LIST AND CHECKING IT TWICE

Your next assignment is to make a log of whom you called or sent packages to and when you did so. Add any extra notes of interest about that submission. You'll be sending out packets and making numerous phone calls, so track all this information along the way. Don't forget to leave enough room on your worksheet for details. You may need to refer to them in your follow-up conversation.

Keep reviewing this list (for your follow-up activity), and keep adding to it. This log is never ending. You should keep it handy for use throughout your career. (Keep it close to those other files you made from earlier assignments.)

As you can see, from the worksheet sample, this type of log is easy to fill out and maintain. Take time to complete the information at the end of each day. Keep this log in a three-ring binder on your desk or in a filing cabinet—anywhere nearby so you can access it at a moment's notice. I sometimes send packages throughout the day, and, without some type of order, I would forget who, what and when in less than a couple of days. It's too easy to tune out who you called or sent things to as time lapses, so set up some type of system to track leads and stay organized. If maintaining the log seems like drudgery, here's an incentive: You'll save at least one to two hours a day using the above method. That adds up to eight hours a week—a whole day! Just think how much more time you'll have to make contacts.

Reward yourself by taking a couple of those saved hours to do something special, even if it's to watch some escape TV or take a leisurely walk. It's important to take time out to compensate yourself in some way for all your hard work.

PLAY THE NUMBERS GAME

When you're looking for the job you want, keep your solicitation process active. Set reasonable goals for yourself. I suggest you contact at least six to twelve people a day, but whatever your magic number, honor your daily goal.

As in anything you go after, finally getting what you want becomes a numbers game. The more you put out there, the more opportunities you create—the more that comes back to you. It's only a matter of time before you get where you need to go to get that job you want.

I know many people who ascribe to this idea. It sounds great, but doing it is quite another thing. Persistence is the key to building a base, and ultimately, securing the job you want. The biggest problem most job seekers have is that they simply run out of steam. And believe me, it's hard to keep tallying up your efforts. There are days when you don't want to honor your goals at all. But force yourself—get disciplined to reach out to new sources every day. I'm a firm believer in the idea that we are creatures of habit. I'm personally grateful to a handful of Dominican nuns: They made me study and instilled a work ethic in me that has stuck. They were big on not giving up on anything.

FOLLOW THE LEAD

Following up with each person you've called or sent a package to is the next practical step in the networking process. You know from your log how much time should elapse before you follow up. When you do make your calls, remember that your mission is to get an appointment or a referral. Try for the appointment, because even if you just want that person as a networking contact, you're

more memorable if you meet in person. Record your progress in the "Comments/Notes" section of your log.

As you go about your follow-up tasks, maintain another file that chronicles your progress with the leads you consider hot. The criteria for "hot" is people who request that you do something active, such as:

- send more samples when you get them
- call back in two weeks when they're interviewing
- call after the holidays when they have time to talk
- call back in a week when they better know their schedule so they can set up a meeting with you.

Keep track of other reasons to follow up with your hot prospects. The guideline for your "hot" log should always be what is termed "a call to action"—in other words, if a lead gives you a reason or a time to get back with them, do it. This reason provides one more opportunity for you to work the lead. Such diligent follow-up, incidentally, could land you the job you want.

See the sample hot log entry on page 51.

Your entries will look different depending on who you contact and what he or she says. The point is to stay on top of your hot file because it usually includes tasks that need immediate attention and repeated follow-up.

The information contained in these records will also get you closer to your goal. Treat it like the treasure chest it is. In fact, it's your future—possibly your immediate one.

TAKE THE MEETING

After all your effort and follow-through, the payoff will most likely be an invitation to a meeting with that person. Remember that most of the

HOT

CONTACT NAME:
Brett Franks

COMPANY:
Dean Witter

PHONE:
(555) 465-9000

WHAT THEY SAID:
Liked my stuff; will talk to
manager re: meeting me

WHAT TO DO:
Send two letters
of reference

WHEN:
Immediately

leads you're working are qualified ones, so many of them should result in some kind of residual benefit.

When you show up for the meeting, have a package in hand in case the person you're meeting with lost the one you originally sent. Be very organized. Know what you want to say, what you want to ask, and more than anything, be prepared to listen. Pay close attention to them—not you—and take notes if the meeting is to secure networking contacts. If it's a job interview, be prepared to take a few notes if they're absolutely necessary (we'll talk about this in more detail in a later chapter), but keep eye contact with them as much as possible. Try not to take up more time than they seem to have, and find a reason to let them know you'll be back in touch. Examples: "I'll call tomorrow with those references you asked for." "I have a business contact I'll call in to you. Is there a good time to call you tomorrow?" "If it's alright with you, I'll call next week to see how your candidate search is going." "I'll call you next spring to let you know who's lined up for the jazz festival." Leaving your meeting open-ended provides an opportunity to nurture an ongoing relationship. You

want to collect relationships like mutual funds; they grow ever more valuable over time.

Consider with care whatever suggestions a networking source gives you during your meeting. All of these suggestions are important or the source would not have taken the time to meet with you and pass them on.

Rule number one: You're at the meeting to make friends and gather insight and information. Make good use of everybody's time. Take all the tips, ideas and hints you can get. If your meeting is with a possible employer, find out where the person's hot buttons are so you can play them—take a hint in this instance, too. One little tip may be enough to land you the job you want. Whatever hints they throw out, jot them down and file them; they may come in handy.

FOLLOW THE YELLOW BRICK ROAD

If you've done each assignment, you probably realize by now that networking is a journey. As a traveler, you need only to follow the road map you're creating for yourself as you go.

Going from source to source is the strategy that gets you to your final destination, but you must follow one lead up with another in order to get there ("there" being the job you want). Caution: Just like a trip, this journey can make you weary. Forget the question you asked as a child: "Are we there yet?" There is no "there yet," so establish that mind-set from the beginning. All through your professional life you're bound to keep traveling. Keep it on the road, look straight ahead and keep after what you've started. Your ability to stay with the follow-up process every day, in some way, is the key and the means for networking. So keep working whatever leads you get.

The way to measure your success is that for every lead you get, make sure it creates another. You will soon learn that networking is never ending. To stay active in the process is insurance that whatever direction you decide to go, as a result of your various professional journeys, you will have amassed enough connections to help get you there.

CAUGHT IN THE ACT

One of the most enjoyable aspects of networking is that you never know what you'll come upon. You may be surprised at how small the world really is, how much you have in common with perfect strangers and how many accidental meetings spawn long-term friendships.

As you diligently create, experience and nurture your networking contacts, enjoy the process; it's designed to be fun. In fact, when you finally land that job you want, you'll find that networking as an ongoing part of your work day is one of the most rewarding parts of being and staying on the job. I think that's true because it's all about people, and no matter how fast technology moves or what it provides, we still need each other. Life has meaning through the relationships we build. That's as true in the workplace as it is with our friends and families.

CHARTING YOUR PROGRESS

Make a file to chart your journey with a graph or an actual geographical map. Lay out a large piece of paper (one that can fold and fit into your binder). Decide whether your spreadsheet will be a map or graph. If it's a graph, tie your contacts (travels) together with bars or lines. If you're making a map (my favorite), draw something that looks like a country—the U.S. will do—and position yourself in one geographical location. Rather than cities and towns, each place you identify will be a person's name. I've had people do this task by placing themselves on one coast and charting their cross-country trek as they go; others have had their coastal starting point and named their final destination at the outset. This second group has filled in the blanks (contact names and companies) step by step as they wove their way toward the opposite coast. Your spreadsheet can also take on the characteristics of a family tree (or one of those corporate management charts) if that visual is easier for you to work with. This assignment is not too different from the concept behind the dot-to-dot game you played as a kid. Have fun with it. I know some people who've actually hung their spreadsheet on the wall and used it as a source of inspiration. I had one friend who did the whole nine yards with little paper doll figures, color-coded pins and little flags. He said it was easier to follow his progress. He was a bank teller wanting to get into the mortgage broker business. I say make a mural if you have a large empty wall. You can always paint over it, possibly as a celebration for getting that coveted job. Make it a party!

ASSIGNMENTS FOR MAKING ACTUAL CONTACTS

1. First, to keep you motivated, write down the three basics: determination, creativity, perseverance. Post this trio in frequently viewed places, i.e., your day planner, bathroom mirror, telephone, etc. Now write down a selection of your favorite affirmations that support these ideals. Post them strategically. Recite them every day—throughout the day—and refer to them whenever you're having a tough moment.

2. Get it together before you get together with that contact. Make a punch list of things you wish to talk to the contact about. Be ready to explain what you need and want, concisely, and be a good listener.

3. Have six packages ready to go at all times.

4. Contact at least six to twelve people each day (Monday through Friday) by either telephoning them or sending your presentation package.

5. Attempt to get a fifteen-minute meeting with each of these contacts, whether you want more connections from them or a job.

6. Take notes when appropriate.

7. Be thankful and gracious. Never be patronizing.

8. Make a log of who you called and sent packages to. Include who, when, where, phone number, follow-up date, comments and notes and names of any leads the person provided. Cross file your leads by adding them to your "Name" file.

9. Keep your log in an accessible three-ring binder or file.

10. Keep your solicitation process active. Honor your preset goals. It's a numbers game; the more you put out the more you get back.

11. Follow up with each lead no sooner than four days and no later than ten days. Make your "Hot" file. The guideline for this file is something someone requested or suggested that shows promise or has a time line attached to it. Include people you need to respond to in some way—soon, or who need repeated follow-up.

12. Be mindful of information you were given during any meeting. People who agreed to meet with you either spent their valuable time to give you pertinent information, or they showed an interest in hiring you. Take all the tips, hints and ideas you can get. Use them to your benefit.

13. Try to leave your meeting open-ended. Leave that door open; set a reason to get together again.

14. The key is your ability to follow up—persevere!

15. Make a map or graph that charts your job journey. Put it in your binder or hang it on your wall. Get creative with it; one of the more fun assignments is tracking your steps to your final destination.

Designed to guide you toward finding and utilizing contacts, the assignments will help you answer questions directly and assist you in keeping track of all leads and your progress with them. You'll be networking day in and day out if you follow what's prescribed here.

chapter seven

Perfecting Your Public Relations

I t doesn't matter how many contacts you accumulate if you don't know how to handle them. If you don't approach them in the right way or if your behavior toward them isn't diplomatic, you may project yourself poorly, precluding you from reaching the contacts you need in the first place. Worse, you may lose your contacts as fast as you get them.

At first blush, networking may sound like an activity of sorts, it's also an art that takes a great deal of social grace and finesse.

I believe the artistic side of networking not only takes intuition, insight and a sense of creative adventure, it also takes superb PR skills and the know-how of what is and what is not, appropriate.

IMAGE IS EVERYTHING

Your public relations is an integral key to opening networking doors. Having been in the public relations field for more than thirty years, I know firsthand how important a good sense of PR is for everyone who is in any business. In my line of work, without good public relations there would be no relations at all. My livelihood depends on my ability to establish and maintain harmonious relationships with those from whom I need something to do my job every day—mainly because all my results as a publicist depend on the connections I make, and more importantly, the connections I keep. What those connections think of me, then, is critical.

Think of public relations as your image—how you project yourself—as well as the manner in which you approach and behave toward others.

It's vital for each of us to have a great sense of PR in terms of image and behavior. I think one of the reasons Bill Clinton won the presidential election the first time out is because he promoted a one-of-the-guys image and had a knack for not seeming pretentious when meeting and greeting others. Winning any election is nothing more than a PR event.

You may not be a politician—you may not even like politicians—but as a job hunter you are trying to get "votes." You're trying to persuade people to help you, whether you're dealing with networking contacts or potential employers—whether you want something from them today, tomorrow or five years from now. Therefore, you need to become PR savvy, which is simply a matter of knowing how to come across and how to behave. You do this by selling an intangible: an image.

WHAT'S YOUR LINE?

Half my work consists of enticing the media to do positive stories on the individuals and companies I represent. My success ratio is how my clients monitor and measure my worth. I'm forever selling intangibles—story ideas and images—and if the media doesn't like or respect me, they won't be interested in my clients. You're selling an intangible in your job search: the image prospective employers get of you. That type of merchandising is an art.

My ability to present myself with integrity, sincerity and professionalism and follow through with that image is foremost in all my dealings. I want these people to like and respect me. Your goal in dealing with those who can make a difference in your business world needs to be the same. I demonstrate my integrity by showing that I am consistent and dependable. I make a conscious effort to be genuinely honest and sincere in all my dealings. Also, I project a sense of professionalism, always trying to say and do the appropriate things and never losing my cool. My follow-through punctuates these traits. I constantly let those with whom I do business know I will do whatever it takes to get the job done.

That's the image I want to project; that's what I want people to think of me as a businessperson, so I make all this a daily habit. It's how I perform. Consistency is a factor as well. It does

little good to be professional one day and slack off the next. Think "image."

The most important line to say (and mean) when coming upon a new contact is: "I'm really glad to meet you." Remember, it's your job to make yourself liked and respected by everyone you come in contact with.

HOW DO YOU RATE?

Go back a week or so and recap the way you approached those to whom you went for help or guidance, and jot down the image you think you projected (e.g., "I thought I appeared confident," "I gave the impression that I was a team player," "I think they liked my laugh"). Next, write down short phrases or descriptions of how you think you behaved toward these people (e.g., "I was friendly but not very attentive to them," "I showed interest in the information they gave me and was polite and thankful throughout our conversation," "I probably shouldn't have told him his Marlin wall hanging was puny").

If you had to guess right now what people think of you—the image you portray—and how good you are in dealing with people, how do you think you'd fare?

When you break it all down, the idea is to always present yourself with a positive spin—with an upbeat, warm approach and an awareness of the impression you're making. Doing all that is a real art, and we're all different in the way we perform this art. Just like any performing artist, it's OK to give it your own personal touch. Maybe you're the type who likes to shake hands firmly while making good eye contact, maybe you like to chitchat a bit when you first meet someone or perhaps your sense of PR calls for trying to find things in common. Just make sure your public relations package is something you continually work on. Find what is distinctively "you" and determine how you can present yourself in a positive and memorable way.

Ultimately, your goal is to please people and make them like you. But PR is a personal thing for both you and the people in your business world. Keep in mind that no two people are alike; what might please one, may not be the hot button for another. Start tuning in to what makes people feel good, and deliver what they seem to need. Think of yourself as a great restaurant server; you want to be hospitable so your tips will be plentiful.

With each new contact, demonstrate diplomacy, courtesy, sensitivity and interest. A personalized touch indicates that you're willing to give back more than you take. This will be very important as you come to count on contacts in your networking circle whose help you need to get that job you want. So go ahead, rate yourself now. Do you please others? If so, how? Do you do it all the time, some of the time or only when you feel like it? What kinds of things do you do to place yourself in a positive light? What could you do to strengthen your image? What do you think people's impression is of you?

The bottom line is to be mindful of how you come across and how you behave with networking contacts and potential employers, whether you want something from them today, tomorrow or five years from now.

BE GENEROUS

When you practice good PR, you find ways to give back more than you get. You take time out to show appreciation; you take notice of what is important to your contacts (what they like and need); you go out of your way to stay in touch for valid reasons. You send an article they would be interested in, titles of books you think they

would like, notices about events or programs of which they've shown interest.

The trick is to do these things not only when it serves your needs, but all the time, expecting nothing in return. Don't think in terms of payback. Don't butter people up just to ask a favor. Believe that good deeds always come back to you, because in the world of networking, they do. Bill Ellermeyer, one of the cutting edge business leaders in my circle, contends that networking is more about giving than getting. He says when you give without any expectation of return, it comes back to you in spades. I have one friend who helps anyone in the business community who approaches her and as far as I know, every single person she helped has repaid her with a valuable referral or lead. She did not expect it; it just happened as the result of her good PR.

When I consciously demonstrate my sense of PR, I put the focus on the other person and what he or she needs. That helps me keep in touch with what's really important: long-term relationships. The philosophy behind good deeds and karma truly has some merit. PR is as PR does.

In my lines of work, I'm forever making friends and acquaintances, hoping each one will remember me in a positive way. I frequently send notes of thanks to the media for hosting or interviewing my clients, and I send thank-you notes to those who have referred business my way. I try to cater to personal or special things I remember about each of my contacts. I attempt to maintain the rapport I've established, and I make rapport-building an ongoing process by staying in touch and giving what I can, without expecting anything in return.

DO IT AGAIN

The mark of a true PR professional is consistency. Whatever practices you put into place, do them as a matter of habit. If it's your PR style to send thank-you notes, send one to every person who helps you in your job hunt. If you have a signature way of staying in touch, like sending humorous tidbits to those who you like and who've helped you, keep it up. Make a list of those "little" things you can do for people on a regular basis; then, make doing them a habit. And always be on the lookout for new ideas. I have a friend who keeps a file of every contact's birthday so she can send them a card with a personal note every year. (That's one of those people pleasers, by the way—we all like to be remembered on our special day.) That's one thing you can do; can you think of others? Make a list of them. Ask your friends for ideas. Make a file folder just for these ideas and act on them regularly.

GIVE SOMETHING BACK

Another way to upgrade your PR skills is for every person who helps you, do something that is geared to get her more business or help her in her job. For example, I work with lots of entrepreneurial consultants, and every time they send some business my way, I find two referrals I can send their way. I'll either call them with the information, send them a note or better yet, ask my referrals to give my consultant friend an introductory call. There is nothing like taking the time to give back to get more. Of course, whenever someone asks me for a referral, I'll mention my friends, but that's a more passive "thank-you." I try to *create* an opportunity, not just take advantage of one.

Of those people who have helped you thus far, have you done something special for them? Each of them is in business. Each of them needs clients or customers. What can you do to show interest, return the favor and cement that bond?

List those clients and ideas. Make sure you keep track of them on computer or paper. If you get overloaded you might send your networking contact the same referral twice!

MAKE NEW FRIENDS BUT KEEP THE OLD

I used to go to a summer camp every year where we sang the song "Make New Friends but Keep the Old/One is Silver and the Other Gold." In the networking world, your contacts are worth their weight in platinum. Unfortunately, I've seen far too many people who forget this—people who step on their earlier contacts to get to what they think are bigger and better ones.

There's nothing wrong with cultivating and growing your networking base—that's actually the whole idea—but don't forget the people who helped you along the way.

Every contact is valuable and should be treasured. If you think this is just a bunch of "nice guy" nonsense, consider the practical benefits of treating people well: The person you bypass this week could be next week's big boss. In networking all contacts are equally important.

Whether you're just starting out in the job market or have been a business professional for years, go back over the roster of people in your networking circle. Have you been in touch with them consistently? Have you bypassed or slighted them in any way? Is it time for you to get back in contact with some of these old friends? If so, what ideas come to mind to give you a good excuse to do so? The message here is don't alienate; accumulate.

DON'T TAKE ADVANTAGE

I know a lot of people who tend to overuse their connections, oblivious to the fact that they impose upon people. This is a delicate area and a very fine art. It is important to know where to draw the line, especially when that line keeps moving, because every situation and every contact is different. Develop certain rules and boundaries for contacting your contacts. Make a conscious decision with each networking contact about when it is and is not appropriate to ask that person for something. How, when and why you approach her should all be considered before picking up the phone or sending a note. For example, I have a very important networking contact within the city redevelopment department where I live. I only contact her when those below her can't assist me. She is always willing to provide me with information or help me resolve a dispute, yet I only call upon her when I consider my need extremely important.

One way to avoid pestering a good networking connection is to be organized and prepared before you approach him. Have your notes in front of you, whether you make contact by phone or in person. There is nothing that annoys me more than someone calling two or three times to say, "Oh, I forgot, just one more thing. . . ." It's not only irritating, it's terribly unprofessional.

Don't call or ask for things often. It's one thing to maintain regular contact with your source; it's another to call with so many requests that they start to feel used. When you ask for too much too often, people will eventually stop returning your phone calls, or they'll begin to avoid you at those chamber of commerce mixers.

Once again, for every one thing someone gives you, give two things back. Before you even make contact with contacts, see if there is something you can do for them right after they've helped you. Send a referral or a useful idea, if possible. It's a great way to say thanks and show

you mean it. When we give back more than we take, people don't mind hearing from us. In fact, they love hearing from us! Far too often, though, I have seen people think only of themselves. They're only in touch when they want or need something. How would you rate yourself right now? Are you bugging people too much? Are they glad to hear from you? Do you take good care of them in little ways?

MIND YOUR MANNERS

If you're having trouble grasping the art of good image projection, call your mother. I'm sure she will happily remind you of the dos and don'ts of good manners. She will probably tell you to sit up straight, smile and say thank you. She will probably also remind you to do unto others as you would have them do unto you. If you can't say anything nice, don't say anything at all, may be another of her admonishments, as well as, it is always better to give than to receive. If your mother isn't around, take a nostalgic pause and see if you can recall her words of wisdom. What's even more fun is to call a sibling and reminisce about some of the things you remember your mother drilling into you.

My mother had an expression, "You made it, you eat it," which originated when my sister and I baked a coffee cake that turned out like cement. Mom told us not to bake it until she got home, but of course, we did it anyway. From that day forward she would repeat that saying (we'd all laugh), but it always meant a great deal to me. Translated, it meant "You reap what you sow." What a perfect lesson when it comes to networking! Make a list of some of the wonderful things your mother said to you and the wonderful things you tell your children (they're probably one and the same). They will guide you as you travel the path to networking success.

WORKSHEET: PERFECTING YOUR PR

1. Make note of the things you say during the course of conversations with networking sources. Remember to be clear, to the point, polite and appreciative, and leave each person with good feelings about you. Try to reconstruct as many conversations as you can.

   The following is a recollection (to the best of my ability) of the most recent conversations I've had with networking contacts:

   _____
   _____
   _____
   _____

   Here is my itemization of things I forgot to say or could have said better during that conversation:

   A) _____
   B) _____
   C) _____
   D) _____
   E) _____

2. Assess your PR image. After each encounter with a contact, describe on paper the image you think you projected. Make a list of things to practice and improve. Describe on paper how you treated that contact, how you probably made him or her feel. Again, make a list of behaviors on which you can improve:

   A) _____
   B) _____
   C) _____
   D) _____
   E) _____

3. In a sound bite, I feel I project this image:_____
   _____

4. I can strengthen and improve that image by:

   A) _____
   B) _____
   C) _____
   D) _____
   E) _____

5. I demonstrate the following behaviors to others to ensure good public relations:

   A) _____
   B) _____
   C) _____
   D) _____
   E) _____

continued

6. I think I could also do these things to please others:

A) _____

B) _____

C) _____

D) _____

E) _____

7. These are some of the creative things I know I can do to provide that personal touch—to say "thank you" or "I care"—to the networking contacts who have helped me:

A) _____

B) _____

C) _____

D) _____

E) _____

8. Make a list of your contacts, old and new, remembering that all networking contacts are equally important. Beside each name, write at least one idea for something—a contact name, the title of a book, a newspaper clipping, a brochure for a seminar—that you can send the person to stay in touch. Over the next few weeks send to the following:

Name of Contact	What to Send
_____	_____
_____	_____
_____	_____
_____	_____
_____	_____

9. Always give back more than you take, and when someone helps you, send something her way immediately. Anyone can say "thank you," but this says you mean it. In view of that, the following include the names of my networking contacts (not to be confused with friends old and new) to date and what referrals or ideas I can provide to help each of them:

Names of Contact	Referrals or Ideas
_____	_____
_____	_____
_____	_____
_____	_____
_____	_____

10. Review your list of contacts, noting when and how often you have asked them for help. Note any contacts you have overused or abused in any way. Come up with ways to make amends.

A) _____

B) _____

C) _____

D) _____

E) _____

continued

11. The following are some ways of demonstrating my social skills when it comes to taking good care of my contacts because I always do the following:

A) _____

B) _____

C) _____

D) _____

E) _____

12. Great ideas for good manners and better behavior toward others can often start with what our mothers told us. The following is a list of the most important things my mother always told me, which I plan to use when dealing with others:

A) _____

B) _____

C) _____

D) _____

E) _____

13. This list includes books I've read or have been suggested to me for reading, that will help me be more aware of appropriate behavior toward those I come into contact with while I build my network pool:

A) _____

B) _____

C) _____

D) _____

E) _____

14. The single most important saying I will remind myself of every day that best describes my perception of the concept of good PR is:

_____

15. In a sentence or paragraph, write down your personal definition of the art of public relations:

_____

_____

_____

_____

_____

_____

_____

_____

_____

_____

_____

Read books such as Robert Fulghum's *All I Really Need to Know I Learned in Kindergarten*, then make notes on the affirmations and lessons that resonate with you. By the time you get done with your mother and your reading materials, you should be PR royalty.

One last thing: When it comes to projecting a positive image and approaching people with finesse and diplomacy, you can't afford to have a bad day. Unfortunately, people remember those negative experiences. Think "Good PR" at all times as you present yourself to the business world.

SUMMARY

You've gained a thorough understanding of the more artistic, diplomatic side of networking. You've helped define your PR image and how you can improve it. You've also been through a refresher course in good manners.

The previous assignments took a great deal of thought and effort. Keep your notes handy as you continue networking; the lessons of good PR are well worth keeping in mind. They will also help prepare you for the next two chapters: Packaging Yourself Appropriately and The Art of Conversation.

chapter eight

Packaging Yourself Appropriately

t's time to put together a presentation that shows you at your best. This package, which for most people will consist of a cover letter, resume and work samples, will be your introduction to would-be employers and the potential leads and contacts you identified in chapters four and five. What goes into this package will differ depending on your experience, background and accomplishments, but in all cases the idea is to make an outstanding first impression.

As you assemble the components of this package, remember that what matters isn't the quantity of materials you cram in, it's the quality with which you present it. Presenting yourself in the most favorable light is critical. Your materials must be professional, easy to comprehend and, more than anything else, just plain simple. Though this may sound like a contradiction, you must be comprehensive but brief; the key is to be specific and substantive without being verbose. Yes, you want to showcase who you are and what you've done, but in terms of pieces

of paper, you don't need many. To inundate is to alienate. No one has time to search through gobs of information to glean what is meaningful; your selling points should be obvious.

Your presentation package is meant to arouse interest and get you in the door. That's all. No potential employer or network contact wants a Movie-of-the-Week of your life and professional times. When people want more, they'll ask. Besides, offering too much tends to look like you're overselling, which hints at insecurity. Your number one priority when presenting yourself is to come across with nonchalant self-confidence. A tight package says, "I'm full pro." It also saves you time and postage. So no matter how many times you update your package, always think, "Less is more."

THAT FIRST IMPRESSION

The three things a potential employer or networking contact needs to receive when you make that all-important first impression are a cover letter, resume and sample or two of your best work. This provides an overview and a reasonable glimpse of who you are, what you've done and what you have to offer. I receive materials every day from friends who pass someone's package on for me to forward to the right person. I also get packages from would-be employees. Nothing irritates me more than having to pore over information to get to the heart of it. By the time I figure out the specifics, I've become resentful. I've also lost interest and am not terribly inclined to pass on the information because my willingness to do so comes across like a recommendation.

Your package is your calling card. It is the first and often the most lasting impression. It is meant to get you in the door. Once you pass through, you can show more samples, provide more information about yourself or expand on the highlights of your character and career. Think of your package from the reader's point of view. If it weren't your own, is it something you would want to read? Be informative and entertaining, brief and concise—think Ernest Hemingway.

WHAT THEY SEE IS WHAT THEY GET

Before I go into the specifics of creating your package, here's a key piece of advice: How you present yourself says a lot about your level of professionalism, and that's the number one quality businesspeople notice. Many will assess your level of self-confidence based on the degree of professionalism you exhibit. The package you send is a clear representation of who you are, so pay strict attention to all the details. Each one of them will tell your reader what league you're in—amateur or professional.

Stationary

Choose the highest quality paper you can afford. No photocopy paper, please. Instead, use a linen bond; you can find some inexpensively at any discount stationers. We send subliminal messages with our materials, and cheap paper can play havoc with "their" sense of "our" self-esteem. Conservative paper color is best. Forget pastels or screaming neon; choose ivory, light gray or light tan—colors that are gentle on the reader's eye. White is okay, too. There's nothing like the crispness of black on white, although a hint of background color is easier on the eyes. And no fancy ink colors—black ink only. Gimmicky colors suggest that your work isn't good enough to speak for itself. Also, make sure your stationary is consistent. Send everything in your package on the same paper if possible. When you use different colors, paper weights and typefaces, your package could be presented like junk mail.

Neatness

No smudges, coffee cup rings or curled corners on your papers. Make sure your package looks clean and crisp. Use an $8'' \times 14''$ envelope so you don't have to fold your material; the package looks neater when it arrives. Don't staple anything together. Just leave each page loose.

Make sure there are no correction fluid marks, cross outs, eraser marks or numbers written over or updated in pen. Make sure you didn't accidentally run your pen across any page; random lines look sloppy. The neater the package, the better the impression you'll make. It's that initial look that makes the difference between someone wanting to meet you and someone deciding instantly that they'll pass. The tidiness of your package is just as important as the information you put inside it.

Proofreading

Nothing says unprofessional more than mistakes in your materials. The reader doesn't know if you made an inadvertent error or if you just can't spell. Most professional jobs require that written materials not be submitted to clients and customers with mistakes in them. Mistakes in your presentation package signal to the receiver that you may not be proficient in spelling, punctuation, or at the very least, proofreading. Going over your materials a few times is always a good idea. And it wouldn't hurt to have someone else take a quick look at what you're sending. Sometimes when we look at something too long we don't catch those little mistakes. In any case, check for errors and correct them. The scrutiny of any final piece is the only foolproof way to avoid embarrassing errors. Whenever I receive a resume or cover letter with an error, I automatically stop reading and throw it away.

Grammar, Punctuation and Spelling

Make certain all these skills are up to par as you put your package together. It will become apparent to your reader that you are not professional if there are misspelled words, bad grammar or inappropriate or missing punctuation. Nearly every position demands good English skills, so don't submit a package that makes someone question your credibility because you're lacking in that area. When I look at a resume, the first thing I notice is spelling. If I see one misspelled word, I toss it. If the sender doesn't care enough to present himself professionally, I don't either.

You can buy several good books to help double-check your English skills, such as William Strunk and E.B. White's *Elements of Style*, the *Scribner Handbook to English* and *The Associated Press Stylebook and Libel Manual*. I urge you to make these books a part of your reference library.

Many computer programs also have grammar and spell-check features on them. They can assist you, but in the end, a final look on your part is the only way to assure that there are no mistakes. As a copywriter, I still proofread my own stuff; I can't rely on my computer's spell-check. A word may be spelled properly but not used properly. For instance, it may tell you if you've misspelled "street" but if you've written "on" when you meant "an," you've got a problem.

Of course, there is nothing like a dictionary and a thesaurus for security. They are two books everyone should have on their desks.

Typewritten Not Handwritten

All materials should be typewritten, not handwritten. Save handwriting for the personal thank-you notes when and where they're appropriate. Even if you don't own a computer, you can borrow one or rent time on one to create your presentation package. Anything in handwriting tells the reader you're not quite professional. Type the name and address in the same typeface you used in your packet of materials. Consistency also says a good deal about your sense of professionalism.

When it comes to typefaces, don't use fancy fonts or a variety of fonts in your package of documents. It, too, bespeaks of unprofessionalism. Some people choose kooky fonts in an overzealous attempt to make an impression. The idea is to submit your package in an understated way. Simple is always best.

Bells and Whistles

Keep in mind that the majority of times you present your package won't be in person. Most likely, someone will pass it on for you, or you will send it by mail. What the receiver reads creates a strong mental picture. You want that visual to be effective and memorable. Ultimately, you want to entice that person into meeting you. Intrigue them!

I have had many prospective employees send me clever teasers. Once a photographer sent me a postcard that displayed half his face in shadow. It made me want to see what he really looked like, so I bit. It was his well-done sample that made me do so. He arrived with five different photos that unfolded the mystery. All revealed, it gave an impressive full face and body shot of him taking a photo. Had he not sent me this interesting sample, I may not have responded. At that time I didn't need additional photographers, but I was interested enough to let him stop by. I ended up hiring him for several jobs, and he is still on my photo roster. What is it you have that is different and creative that you can forward with your package? Remember that the people you're targeting receive things all day. Make your package stand out.

Having said all that, I want to caution you that there is a thin line between being clever and being hokey. It would be better not to do something outstanding if you're not absolutely certain it's appropriate. Only take the chance of sending something very different if you think it's interesting and tasteful, not overbearing. The idea is to stand out, not get thrown out!

But Did I Ever Show You My . . . ?

Don't fret over all the things you want someone to see. If they like your first presentation, you'll be able to send an additional one. Most often, you'll have the opportunity to present your follow-up materials in person, just like the photographer I just mentioned.

Here's another example—my own. I was once a strong candidate to become a staff writer for the Fox TV sketch-comedy show, *In Living Color*. My first impulse was to send every funny sketch I had ever written. However, my agent told me to select my two strongest pieces. If they liked those, he advised, they would ask for others; if I gave them too much, they would "pitch the package." "We just want to make a powerful first impression," he said. And he was right. They came back for more. They did ask for other samples, and they asked me to write a few pieces expressly for the characters on the show. By the time it looked like I might get the gig, the show had political problems and folded. But I had made a good impression, which was extremely important to me. What I learned is that if someone wants more, they will ask. A tighter package saves you time, postage and screams, "I'm full pro!"

CONSISTENCY

One of the key points I stress when I coach people in public speaking and communication is to present a consistent image, whether in person or on paper.

You must ask yourself: Am I consistent in my presentation? Is my package always my personal best? It is a small world and people talk, so all presentations are equally important. You probably have been surprised to find out that your contact person or prospective employer knows so and so. These people may share information about you or talk about their experience with you. You always want to go for consistent quality, because you never know whose path may cross with someone else's. Consistency also demonstrates your level of integrity and professionalism.

I learned this early from the acting coach I had as a preteen. I hated her for it at the time, because it seemed she reminded me how important consistency was at every lesson. The idea reverberates each time I go before a client, audience or group. There are days when I don't feel like putting forth my best, but there is no margin for mood swings. I don't want people who talk about me to say things like, "Oh, I guess she was having an off day; her speech wasn't as good as the last time I saw her." I would die if that happened. I'm trained to be the most solid professional I can whenever I encounter those in the business world.

As part of that consistent image, don't ever let them see you sweat, cry or pitch a fit. If you have a bad day, don't take it into the professional arena with you; it may be the day you meet a very important person—a contact you need referrals from or a potential employer. If a potential boss asks a networking contact about you, you certainly don't want that contact to have anything negative to relay.

So as you travel through various networking circles and meet people for whom you may want to work, remember that the circle is not so large. If you're consistent in your presentation and professionalism, people will only say good things about you—consistently.

COVER LETTERS

Your cover letter should be concise, have a logical flow and be only one page long (the shorter, the better). Don't be redundant. Your letter should be no more than four to six paragraphs. You don't need to tell them more than what is contained in that much space. Don't say something in the cover letter that is mentioned in your resume.

Be careful of your wording. Don't use phrases like "I hope to hear from you"; instead use "I look forward to hearing from you." Instead of "I desperately want to work in this field," say "I am eager to work in this field." Your wording is part of your image. If you sound the

least bit needy or insecure, people will pick up on that. At the same time, you don't want to sound egotistical, either. Saying things like, "I'm the best at coming up with ideas," "No one can perform better than me," "Everyone has always told me I was the greatest accountant" or anything that sounds like bragging is another turn-off.

Finally, don't sound heavy-handed. I always resent the letters that close with, "I'll contact you to find a mutually convenient time to get together." A better way to word it is, "I'll contact you to find out when it will be convenient for you to meet with me." The former sounds very arrogant, yet I see cover letters like this all the time. Make certain you come across as confident but not cocky. Check your words and phrases carefully. You should sound respectful and courteous, businesslike and professional.

The following are examples of cover letters. The first is geared toward a prospective employer; the second is written to a network contact. Both are written as though the writer has not yet spoken to the party but has been referred by a mutual contact. Next, I will provide samples of letters written after an initial conversation, when you're sending your package.

As you can see, the following letters are direct and simple. They are designed for a quick read and state only the pertinent information. Letters like the aforementioned are all you need. You want to come across as professional and businesslike, but also human and connectable. Your letters should be the first step in establishing rapport. It's okay to come across as friendly and upbeat. I see far too many letters that go to the extreme of formality. I believe that's a turn-off, especially when you're trying to build a networking base. People want people. You want

Letter # 1: Prospective Employer

March 22, 1999

Mr. Paul Driskell
TLC Services
1213 17th Street
Santa Ana, CA 92706

Dear Mr. Driskell:

My name is Josh Whitner, and I'm writing to you today at the suggestion of Linda Edwards, to express my interest in working for TLC services.

For the past three years, I have worked as an accountant for two trucking companies, Condor Freight Lines and Osterkamp Trucking. At Condor, where I served as the head of accounting, I handled all accounts payable and receivable and managed three subordinates. At Osterkamp, I was responsible for managing the purchase orders for all buying transactions, as well as gathering all quotes and bids from outside vendors.

I'm currently seeking a position with a company that offers growth potential, a professional challenge and a team atmosphere. Linda said TLC fit that profile perfectly.

I am hardworking and truly enjoy solving difficult problems. I like to organize and implement new programs, and I am extremely positive in my approach to any work-related challenge. My attached resume further describes my abilities, background and experience.

I would certainly welcome the opportunity to meet with you at your earliest convenience to discuss how my experience and capabilities might be a compatible fit with your current professional needs. I can be reached at (555) 676-3345.

Thank you for your time and consideration. I look forward to speaking with you soon.

Sincerely,

Josh Whitner

Letter #2: Network Contact

March 22, 1999

Mr. Paul Driskell
TLC Services
1213 17th Street
Santa Ana, CA 92706

Our mutual friend, Linda Edwards, suggested I contact you regarding the possibility of meeting with you, on the phone or in person, to discuss potential contacts you may have who might be interested in hiring me.

By way of a quick overview, I have been in the accounting field for the past three years and have extensive experience in all facets of accounting procedures. I've enclosed for your review a resume detailing my experience and capabilities.

I'm currently looking to join a company that offers growth potential, challenge and a strong team atmosphere. I am diligent and committed to problem-solving; I enjoy implementing new programs and approach every work-related situation in a positive manner.

I realize you're extremely busy, but I would much appreciate a short visit to jot down possible names and companies who may be looking for someone like me. If I haven't heard from you within a few days, I'll give you a call to see if we can get together.

Thanks so much for your time thus far. If there is some way I can be of service to you, please don't hesitate to let me know. I look forward to talking to you soon.

Kindest regards,

Josh Whitner

relationships; remember, they are the heartbeat of your professional lifeline.

The preceding letters were "cold letters"— the sender never met the receiver. As you begin to network, you will write your share of such letters, but you will also write to potential employers or contacts you have already met.

As you will see, the following two letters are a little more casual, since Geraldine has already met and spoken to Paul McGrath. Remember the key when coming into contact with others: Make the human connection!

THE RESUME

The key to creating a professional, impressive resume is to put yourself in the reader's shoes. You are asking someone to absorb a lot of specific information—names, dates, places, positions—so you want to make it digestible. Your resume should be one page only. I don't care how much background you have, no one wants to read a two-page (or more) dossier. Again, people get materials all day, everyday; they need to travel through your package quickly, all the while getting a strong, positive picture of who you are, what you've done and what you have to offer.

Though there are various ways to prepare one, be careful that yours is easy to read and provides pertinent information at the outset. Since he was young and hadn't been in the workplace very long, a friend of mine listed his information with "Education" first, then "Work Experience," followed by "Special Interests." I recommend starting with a short, explanatory paragraph with the heading, "Objective." This sound bite should clearly state your job interest and intent.

Your resume layout—margins, indents, typefaces, typestyles (bold, caps or italics)—should be consistent so it has a professional look.

When listing job descriptions, be careful that you don't mix titles with activities. If you're going to say you were a "Production Supervisor" at one job, don't start the next item on your resume with "Supervised production." Use titles or job descriptions, but not both. Watch for consistency in how you describe each work experience.

Always list your "Work Experience" in order of last job first. Don't get too wordy explaining each job; keep things simple and go for the highlights (keep thinking sound bites). The more intricate you get, the more bored the reader becomes. You should include short, snappy descriptions. For instance, you don't want to say:

Production Supervisor: In this job I oversaw all major jobs from beginning to end, I filled out reports about how the jobs were completed and I handled and wrote out all the needed items on the budgets for each job.

Instead, try this:

Production Supervisor: Prepared budgets, oversaw all facets of production and prepared detailed reports on production details.

That's enough explanation and far easier to understand. You want the explanations under each job assignment to show your abilities and sense of responsibility. That's enough. Also, you need only list your last three or four positions, or provide an overview in terms of chronology of your career highlights.

Next, you can list "Special Talents, Interests, Awards," only if they viably add to your credentials. Mention, as a tag, that references are available upon request, but don't bother listing them

Letter #1: Prospective Employer

April 4, 1999

Mr. Paul McGrath
PTC Industries
400 Balboa Ave.
Colorado Springs, CO 80922

Dear Paul:

It was really great meeting you last week at the Chamber mixer and getting the opportunity to talk a bit about PTC. I was glad to learn that you may be looking to hire someone with my skills and experience. It sounds like my joining PTC could be a win for both of us!

Per your request, I've enclosed some background information on myself.

Let me know if you would like to meet soon. I will be happy to bring along additional samples of my work and a list of references.

If there is anything else you need, please let me know.

By the way: Wasn't that a great speaker?

Kindest regards,

Geraldine McIntosh

Letter #2: Network Contact

April 4, 1999

Mr. Paul McGrath
PTC Industries
400 Balboa Ave.
Colorado Springs, CO 80922

Dear Paul:

What a fortunate chance dinner meeting for me last week!

As I mentioned to you over the rubber chicken, I have been working on building a network base to establish job contacts who might be interested in finding someone like me—an eager and enthusiastic business-supplies salesperson—to add to their staff.

I appreciate your interest in my background package (which I've enclosed) and your willingness to pass it on to the people we talked about.

Per your suggestion, I will call in a few days to get their names and phone numbers so I can follow-up.

In the meantime, if there is anything I can do for you, please consider adding my name to your network base.

Thanks again, Paul. I appreciate your time and effort.

Warmest regards,

Geraldine McIntosh

on your resume or enclosing any letters of recommendation. If an employer or network contact needs or wants them, he'll ask.

I believe the following sample resumes do the job. When I showed a variety of resumes to two owners of personnel agencies, these two were the hands-down winners in format and content. Notice how simply stated and well organized the information on each document is.

The second resume is a straightforward account of the life of a woman who took time off to raise a family. Rather than dance around the issue, she skillfully made use of her experience during that period of her life to increase her knowledge of running an operation. Rather than play down that part of her life, she proudly and honestly used the information to illustrate her productivity and organizational abilities. Going to school and running a household with three small children are no easy tasks. Note that her resume, too, was simple and to the point.

SAMPLES

Make sure your carefully selected sample (if you include one) is a strong representation of your talent. For instance, if you were selling yourself as a copywriter, you might send a copy of an authored article than ran in a newspaper or newsletter. A secretarial or administrative assistant might enclose a sample letter drafted on behalf of his former boss. A graphic artist might showcase piece a piece of artwork or a slick of a brochure cover. An accountant might include a list of clients or a copy of a creative accounting plan devised for a client. Even if you just graduated, you can share something that illustrates something special about yourself. Be sure your sample makes the person viewing it say, "Wow, that's impressive."

Don't feel compelled to include a sample if you don't have something suitable, and never include one "for the heck of it." Samples are meant to back up what you say in your cover letter and/or resume and leave the reader of your package wanting more. Think of your sample the same way you would an attractive book cover: If you like what you see, you want to look inside to see even more.

As I said earlier: The biggest mistake job candidates make is to pile too much info into their packages. Temper your enthusiasm with some objectivity, and keep things simple. Many personnel managers say they get a strong impression from the package they receive and the samples in it, and that too much is not only tiresome, but suggests a big ego or a person with little confidence. So give very careful thought to what you send. One friend puts his package together and then sets it aside for a day or two. Then, he pretends to be the person who will open it. Through an objective eye he gets a sense of whether or not the package wows him. If not, he starts the process all over again. He told me that the single biggest mistake he makes is that his package is overloaded. I think we all get overzealous in wanting to show our best. But, as the saying goes: Less is more.

YOUR PACKET

Now that you've had the opportunity to review a few sample cover letters, some basic resumes, and to get a feel for what is and is not a suitable sample, it's time for you to prepare your package. Grab a pencil for the following worksheet. You may be making changes as you go.

Cover Letter Worksheet

Make a list of the basics about yourself you want people to know. Itemize your professional abilities, personal qualities, special talents, job titles

CHARLES CARNELLO

2160 Seaward Drive

Niagara Falls, New York 14304

(555) 236-9856

OBJECTIVE

To affiliate with a company that could utilize my vast experience in marketing and promotion as it relates to managing and directing large departments.

WORK EXPERIENCE

3/87–9/98

MOORE BUSINESS FORMS, Buffalo, New York

Vice President/Marketing

- Managed two hundred marketing reps who were responsible for selling products worldwide
- Designed, created and implemented the company's marketing programs

2/80–2/87

MONARCH BUSINESS SYSTEMS, Toronto, Ontario, Canada

Marketing Director

- Trained and supervised fifty sales reps
- Assisted vice president of sales with the design of all company marketing campaigns
- Responsible for creating concepts to introduce each marketing campaign

1/75–2/80

SHAMROCK ADVERTISING, Pittsburgh, Pennyslvania

Marketing Rep

- Called on agency clients to pitch new campaigns
- Collaborated with creative team to package marketing programs
- Assisted marketing director with concepts and campaign ideas

EDUCATION

COLUMBIA UNIVERSITY, New York City

Bachelor of Arts, Marketing and Advertising, June, 1979

- Graduated cum laude—third in my class
- Dean's List
- Recipient of the "Call Up" Award for outstanding creativity

AFFILIATIONS

- Council of World Hunger
- National Association of Marketing Directors
- Panel for Marketing Arts—Marketing League

SPECIAL INTERESTS

- Skiing
- Theater
- Karate

REFERENCES AVAILABLE UPON REQUEST

Sue McDowell
7016 Mountainside Grove
Colorado Springs, Colorado 80922
(555) 596-4562

Objective: To join a dynamic, forward-thinking company that will take full advantage of my capabilities, both as an administrator and executive assistant.

WORK HISTORY: 5/93—6/98	PROFESSIONAL HIATUS Homemaker As a single mother, I cared for three small children, ran a household and studied courses in administrative management to prepare me to re-enter the job market when my youngest entered kindergarten. My sense of efficiency, my ability to be task- and results-oriented and my organizational abilities helped me to further my skills as an excellent administrator.
5/91–5/93	DELL COMMUNICATIONS, Grand Junction, Colorado Administrative Assistant I assisted three vice presidents in their day-to-day sales presentations by preparing their materials, scheduling appointments and formatting and documenting their recap reports. I also researched various competitors and submitted reports on my findings to the management team.
6/85–5/91	HOST FOOD SERVICES, INC., Boulder, Colorado Administrative Coordinator I handled all vendor purchase orders, scouted for food representatives, assisted in company presentations to potential clients and implemented the company's first focus group.
EDUCATION:	UNIVERSITY OF COLORADO, Boulder, Colorado Bachelor of Arts, Business and Administration Graduated April 1984
HONORS:	*Sorority president—Kappa Alpha Theta *Dean's List *Business Department—Student of the Month
REFERENCES:	Both personal and professional—upon request
SALARY:	Negotiable

and job responsibilities, educational degrees, special training, military service, public service—you should be jotting down anything from your past that adds up to the sum of your work experience. Personal information, such as serving on volunteer committees for the local food bank, are equally important. Next, clarify what you want to do professionally and state it. Finally, add what is unique and special about you and your experience that would make someone want to meet you. As you compile this information into cover letter format, you will condense what is important, eliminate what doesn't seem to fit and mention only what would be pertinent to the reader. The following questions will get you started:

1) Who I am _____
2) What I've done _____
3) What I have to offer _____
4) What I'm looking for _____

Compose a letter with those ideas in mind. Keep it direct, simple and easy to read. Do a sample letter to prospective employers and one to potential network contacts. Write cold letters and letters to people you've already met. Run these letters by someone you respect to get their reaction and input. You may need a few finishing touches and an outside objective opinion is always helpful.

Be Prepared

Always make sure you have an ample supply of packages on hand. Don't let your stash get down to less than six on any one day. There will be those days when you get several requests in one day and you don't want to keep anyone waiting.

Once you've assembled a package you can be proud of, make sure you update it on a regular basis. It's unprofessional when you send a resume and say something in your cover letter like: "Since compiling my resume, I have also done so and so. . . ." Stay on top of achievements and experiences that are important enough to highlight. Keep your resume on computer disk—yours or someone else's—so it is easy to update.

Your presentation package is only meant to get you in the door. Save the rest for the next time or the appropriate time.

If you have a business card that includes a phone number or address where someone can easily reach you, include it. But don't give a card with information that is likely to become outdated soon. I had a friend who blew two great job opportunities because her contacts were trying to reach her at a place she no longer worked. If your business card has a pager number, an E-mail address and a cell phone number—places where you can be reached long term—by all means enclose it. But if there is any chance that the information will be obsolete in a year or so, think twice. You may lose out. Better to send a resume with a home phone number. If you move, you will probably have the foresight to arrange for a forwarding referral. Think ahead. You want people to be able to contact you long term.

Presentation Package Cheat Sheet

1. In most cases you need only three documents in your presentation package: a cover letter, resume and sample of your work.
2. Keep your contents concise and to the point. Remember your objective is to give people the highlights of who you are, what you've done and what you have to offer.
3. Make sure all presentation materials are error-free and neatly typewritten or

YOUR RESUME WORKSHEET

Start putting your resume together by making a list of the following. For those of you who already have a resume, check to see if the information is presented simply and concisely, providing only the necessary highlights. Brainstorm for awhile and scribble down all your highlights. Remember there is only one piece of paper to convince potential employers that you have what they're looking for.

1. List your vitals (name, address, phone, etc.) _____
_____

2. My job objective is _____

3. List your job history, the last three or four positions only. Not too many people will care what you did during the summer, in high school or college. Don't leave gaping holes. The reader will wonder what you were doing during the missing period of time. Don't forget the most recent work achievements are the most important. Choose only those historical events of positive impact and recent importance.
A) _____
B) _____
C) _____

4. The following is a list of the job titles I have held during my professional career:
A) _____
B) _____
C) _____

5. Based on the aforementioned job titles, a brief description of each position I've filled includes the following:
A) _____
B) _____
C) _____

6. My education, special training, etc. includes
A) _____
B) _____
C) _____

7. My honors and special commendations include
A) _____
B) _____
C) _____

8. If you're set on a particular salary, list your range. This can be tricky because you might disqualify yourself by asking for too much, or your potential employer may have offered more than what you stated. So be careful with this one.

computer-printed in black ink on linen stock. All materials must be clean and crisp. No slop.

4. Make sure your cover letters are business-like yet friendly. Don't forget the human factor; it's the key when starting to build your network base.

5. Save your trunk of samples for another day. Gloat over them with your family and friends. Pick only one for your prospective employer or network contact.

6. Make sure you have enough materials on hand for those busy days when everyone seems to want your package at the same time.

7. Make sure your business card, if you enclose one, is usable long term.

8. Smile! The hardest part is done. You've got your materials in hand, and you're ready to present yourself.

chapter nine

The Art of Conversation

The need to talk to people—those you already know and those you will be meeting for the first time—is essential to your networking skills. How you talk to people will make the difference as to whether or not you make and keep a networking contact or get the job you want.

If networking is the vehicle to steer you toward the job you want, then communication is the tool that helps you land it. If you don't express yourself effectively, you can't make that human connection. Nor can you sell yourself, and we must all sell to get what we want.

RAPPORT AT THE CORE

As you approach networking contacts and prospective employers, the first thing you want to do is create a sense of rapport. Rapport is an interesting word; Webster's defines it as "relation marked by harmony." In my years of communication skills training, I've described it as a vibe, a good feeling between human energies. Dr. Kappas, the psychologist I referred to ear-

lier, tells his students that rapport is comprised of three elements: trust, like and respect. I think he's nailed it as it relates to the business world. With these three basics in place, all things are possible—especially in making valuable, long-lasting networking relationships and appealing to prospective employers.

As you communicate with others, strive to establish rapport from the very first encounter—no matter who they are. Think about building on its foundation, for through the nurturing and maintenance of relationships our business world turns. To make our way successfully we need strong relationships. Rapport lies at the core of our communication expertise.

TO EACH HIS OWN

Everyone you come in contact with will require a unique touch. Why? Because everyone is different and every situation is one of a kind. You want to be prepared for the unexpected. Always have that mind-set before you approach any contact. Each piece of communication is unique, therefore your conversations will never be one size fits all.

Nothing is worse than hearing someone on the other end of the phone sound as though they are reading from a script, or meeting someone in person with a preplanned list of lines. People who are not spontaneous and alert usually come across as boring and detached. It's as though they have organized everything they thought they might have to say, with no consideration for a sudden abrupt change in the direction of the conversation.

Truth is, we all need to focus on building rapport as we engage in networking conversations. With rapport comes meaningful relationships, and those relationships equal a networking base. It's through a substantive base of contacts that we get that job we want.

As I present the following lessons, be aware that you will run into different types of individuals, their different ways and different days. Be ready to offer up the best communication skills you can muster.

EXPECT THE UNEXPECTED

Be prepared to handle every piece of communication in an individual way. You need to be geared for the unexpected; I guarantee that's what you'll always get.

The people you are about to talk to will span a variety of backgrounds and circumstances, but most of all, people you call for networking purposes (or those you interview with) are going to be unpredictable. How's that? Because you never know what mood they'll be in. Some will be rushed or intently involved in their own stuff, some may feel you're imposing upon them, and some may not be in a mental state to shift gears from what they're doing. Your job is to be ready to field any dialogue that comes your way and

to be able to read people. Each time you converse, do it with intelligence, courtesy, poise, presence and, quite often, humor.

TALK IT UP

Most of us talk up a storm when we're comfortable, improvising everything we say. When we're among friends and family we rarely stop to ponder each word that comes out of our mouths. We just rattle on. When we're among strangers, though, and those who we perceive as being important for some reason (like possible employers), we tend to lose that sense of ease and that spark of spontaneity.

Improvisational comedy actors are never lost for words. They seem to handle every verbal crisis that comes their way. What do improv actors know that we don't? Nothing that you can't learn!

Perhaps many of you have had the enjoyment of watching improv comedy being performed—actors doing scenes based entirely on audience suggestions. It looks so complex, when in fact it is simply the utilization of pre-agreed communication guidelines that guarantee their communication will work each and every time.

How do they work?

I've been teaching and directing improv actors for years, and before any one of them takes to the stage, they are put through the rigors of a "mental boot camp." They are taught a collection of rules and tools that will assure all their communications are fail-safe.

Though improv actors are often perceived as specially endowed with conversational prowess that others don't have, that is just not true. We're all able to do what they do; we just need to learn the tricks of their trade.

I don't think it's necessary to provide you with an entire improv workshop in this chapter, but I will introduce you to improv's basic philosophy and teach you a handful of it's preliminary precepts. You will see why the actor's "scenes" are always so successful and why their conversations inherently work. You, too, can use what they use and implement such principles into every conversation you have, no matter who it's with and where it is.

BEGINNING, MIDDLE AND END

Every scene an improv player engages in must have a beginning, middle and an end. That's a rule. And in most cases, their scenes don't last more than a couple of minutes. That will hold true for you, too, as you create and engage in your scenes—your verbal exchanges with the people you're about to call on. Many of them will be short and sweet. It's important that you first "situate your audience"—provide them with who, what, why, where and when. Give them an idea of who you are and what you are seeking.

Next, you'll move to the middle of the scene. In an improv setting, that means we begin to deal with the conflict or the mission—the purpose or need for the communication (scene) in the first place. Once we make that segue, we know we've hit the middle. In your case, the "middle" will let the person know you're ready to address a remedy or solution relative to your reason for calling in the first place. In other words, once they're situated, it's time to get to the heart of the matter—to find an answer to the need.

In improv, once we have resolved the situation, whatever it is, we're ready to find an ending. We bring resolution to every scene to allow for closure. Once you've arrived at that point, you will be ready to find an ending. For instance, one typical ending for you may be agreeing to send a package, setting a time to meet, suggesting a time to call them back to follow-up or a verbal summary of what suggestions they offered. A "thank you" and "good-bye" will cap off any ending, but before you reach that point, your ending must bring closure and resolve the situation satisfactorily.

You have probably never thought about your conversations requiring a beginning, middle and an end. But from now on, I want you to. It's one way to keep your communications clear, to the point and complete. It bolsters the rapport factor as well, because it lets the other person know you are organized in your communications, you know what you want, how to state it and how to bring any conversation to a productive ending.

TALKING WITH THEM IN MIND FIRST

Two of the three basic overall rules I want you to think about during every conversation are "Serve and Support" and "React and Respond."

Serve and Support is a precept whereby improv actors ask themselves what they can do to take care of the other actors on stage. They take the focus off themselves and pay attention to what the other actors are saying and doing, catering to the others' ideas. Never do they come from their own agenda. Never do they think of themselves. Instead, they only think of taking care of the other person's needs. Because they are so intent on giving way to the other actors, the harmony in their work is astounding. To serve and support is an unselfish way to behave with others. When all the actors are on stage in this same mode, the synergy is unbelievable. You will automatically listen better and perceive people more astutely if you remember to put the focus on the other person. You can play off them in conversation, beautifully. Serving and supporting the other guy doesn't mean you can't get your points across, ask questions or be mindful of why you approached someone in the first place; it's just that as you communicate with them you think of them first and yourself second.

The **React and Respond** theory is a natural segue from the Serve and Support rule. This rule calls for you to react and respond to the last thing said or last idea held. That's all. No thinking or dwelling on the immediate past, no projecting or anticipating the future. No thinking about yourself, necessarily. You just react to the last thing said or last idea expressed. "It's just like playing tennis," says Michael Gellman, director of Second City in Chicago (he has been a resident director and teacher for that organization for three decades). "You just wait to see how the ball comes at you and hit it back accordingly." Wait to see what someone says or does, then react appropriately.

If we could first serve and support—put the focus on the other guy—then react and respond off what they say, we would have tighter communication with others. The other people don't even have to know what rules you're following, either. If you communicate with these rules in mind, they will probably follow suit. If not, you can still verbally go where they go. You can still make all your conversations work because, at a minimum, the two of you are always on the "same page."

As you make your calls and meet people in person, remember to serve and support and react and respond. It will make a terrific difference to both you and them!

STAY IN THE MOMENT

Be Here Now is rule three and quite possibly the most important rule of all. It's also the one all improv players have pounded into them from their very first onstage workout. Be here now means you are never anywhere but in the moment currently transpiring. You're not jumping ahead or lagging behind; you're always in the present. It takes great alacrity to do this, but over time, you will develop the same discipline as that of an improv actor. Through a new awareness of this idea, your listening skills and ability to concentrate and focus will improve. You will manage to stay current throughout the course of each and every conversation. Soon you will find that you process information differently. Rather than thinking, you'll be responding spontaneously, and as a result, appropriately. Robin Williams and so many other great improv actors have mastered this. Their ability to *consistently* "be here now" is what makes them so brilliant.

NEVER REFUSE—NEVER DENY

There is nothing that diminishes rapport faster than ignoring or putting down another person's idea. That goes for every conversation you have, every "scene" you're in. In improv, this is called **Refusal and Denial**—the only two things forbidden in an improv setting.

To refuse is to ignore something someone says; to deny is to change or undercut what someone else is doing or saying. Improv actors are mandated to go with the flow, to acknowledge whatever another actor says or does and, in that process, to not put down or discredit any actor's ideas or actions.

Let me present two quick examples:

Refusal. If I say to you, "Gee I really like you in that green shirt," and you say, "Did you notice my shoes?" you have just refused me. In other words, you have completely ignored what I have said—in effect, bypassed me. I'm left hanging with my idea. There is no direct React and

Respond. A more appropriate response on your part would be, "I'm glad you like me in green, thanks, and oh, did you notice my shoes?" If you do ignore me, we will continue talking perhaps, but probably in the form of two different conversations. You can imagine the outcome of such poor communication. Also, when you ignore someone, you show disrespect and a lack of consideration. You also isolate yourself from them. None of this builds rapport, which is your chief assignment. I have seen people talk for long periods of time, one ignoring the other. You would swear they weren't engaged in the same conversation. Most mistakes made in this area are because people are preoccupied with their own thoughts and agenda. And there's no question that they're not listening all that much.

Denial. If I say to you, "Gee, I really like you in that green shirt," and you say "I hate this shirt, it's stupid," you have just denied me. You have diminished my opinion and invalidated how I think or feel. In an improv setting, whenever you deny someone, you literally bring the scene to a screeching halt. It means you have to start the communication again from scratch by means of a new idea—a kick start of some kind. Sometimes there is no retrieving the piece; it just crashes. We always tell our actors to go in the direction the scene is going by *adding information* to the last thing said or last idea held (react and respond) to keep the conversation alive and moving forward in the same vein. So if I say "Gee, I really like you in that green shirt," you might say, "I'm glad you like me in green even though I'm not terribly comfortable in this color," or "Thanks. Other people say the same so I guess this color works for me." This is a classic example of not denying the other person, and as you can see in the first retort, I can still have a different opinion about myself in

the green shirt. Scenes performed in this manner are guaranteed to work, whether in improv or real life. In improv, audiences don't care if the scene is funny or not, they're just glad to see tight and interesting conversation with the emphasis on good communication. Our real-life scenes can be one and the same.

TOOLS THAT WORK

Consider the use of some of the improv actor's rules and tools as you communicate. I think the way the improv actor is taught to communicate is the purest form of interaction available on the planet. There is almost something holy about it! Whatever their conversations, their scenes (communications) *always* work.

With this at the forefront of your thinking, let's take a look at some of the conversations you may have—what makes them crash and what makes them get you what you want and need.

The scenes in this chapter will cover each type of communication you will probably come up against as you build and maintain your networking base. Some may seem exaggerated, but all make important points.

Your conversations will undoubtedly include the following categories:

- people you've never talked to before, but those you need to talk with to get your networking process started
- people you know only slightly (maybe you've met them once)
- people you know but don't talk to on a regular basis
- people you know well and talk to fairly often

What's the most constructive way to handle each of the above? Well, before I present a breakout from each type of situation with a "before" and "after" sample conversation, there are some basics you'll want to master to ensure each conversation you have showcases you as a true professional. Being professional means you are always clear in your requests, articulate in your responses, a good listener, upbeat, positive, sincere and polite. It also means every conversation you have will produce a positive outcome.

COLD CALL

Our first sample scene deals with approaching individuals whom you have never talked to. Maybe it is someone you discovered in the phone book, maybe it's a name you read in the business section of the local paper. It could be any of those people whose names you collected in the adventure exercise—who you thought could help in your networking quest but who you have never talked to before. Your job is to make a phone call and, starting from scratch, create a relationship.

Let's say you're looking for a job in the aircraft industry. You find the idea of manufacturing airplanes intriguing, and your background and skill level fit the profile of several job possibilities in that field. You decide to call Boeing because they are one of the largest airplane manufacturers in the world. You manage to charm the receptionist who forwards you to the personnel department. Your focus is to network—to originate your first source, knowing it can lead to another. Here's a first take on such a conversation. (Note: "PD" stands for personnel director.)

TAKE ONE:

PD: Hello.

JIM: (Nervous) Hi. I'm trying to get a job in the aircraft manufacturing industry. What job opportunities do you have?

PD: (Obviously caught off guard) What . . . job opportunities . . . ?

JIM: Openings. I mean, jobs, I mean . . . opportunities . . . I mean . . .

PD: We don't have any openings at the present time.

JIM: Oh. You don't?

PD: No, we don't.

JIM: Ya' know who does?

PD: (Impatient) No, not really.

JIM: (Discouraged) OK, thanks.

PD: Sure.

No rapport has been established in this scene; no sense of warmth, no human touch, no situating the audience, little Serve and Support. In terms of React and Respond, it leaves a great deal to be desired. I'll give some credit to Jim for being in the moment, but that's about it. This scene is weak because it lacks a sound beginning, the middle is foggy and the end brings little, if any, resolution to the prescribed assignment (to get contacts). But this is often what happens when you're flustered and nervous and don't know what to say to someone you've never talked to before and who has no idea who you are. Somehow, many people in this awkward position tend to feel submissive and in the process come off insecure. They also can't seem to get their thoughts together. Many people tell me they feel almost light-headed when confronted with such a situation.

But you can get around this. Your job, if you're Jim in this scene, is to set a goal. Your first and foremost goal should be to establish rapport. If you're told there are no jobs, you want to get names of contacts who either have job openings or who can guide you toward them.

Although Jim didn't mean it, he seemed to have an off-putting attitude in this conversation;

he considered himself the center of the universe.

You can portray confidence while remaining humble. You don't have to be meek, and a little humility goes a long way. We all like it in other people. Another note of caution: The "me-first" approach can convey a hint of arrogance—one of the biggest turn-offs in any first-time communication. Another major problem with this conversation is that no introductions were made. How impersonal! Without a human connection there's no chance for rapport; no rapport, no relationship; no relationship, no network and so it goes. Another director's note: Never use slang like "ya' know"; it just doesn't sound professional.

Let's say this time around the only focal point will be on making a relationship happen. With that in mind, let's take another run at the same conversation and see what happens, especially when we follow some of the improv communication guidelines and when our goal is to create rapport and get contacts.

TAKE TWO:

JIM: (Friendly, courteous, upbeat, energetic and confident) Hi, my name is Jim Jones. I'm looking for a job in the aircraft manufacturing industry. I've got great credentials as a maintenance engineer and wondered if I could take a minute of your time to ask a few questions.

PD: Well, I am busy, but well, go ahead.

JIM: I'm sorry, I didn't get your name.

PD: Rachel Smith.

JIM: Oh, hi Rachel.

PD: Hi.

JIM: I love your industry and I'm trying to break into it. Would you happen to have any openings?

PD: Not at the present time.

JIM: (Slight chuckle) Ah, I was hoping you wouldn't say that! Well, then would you be so kind as to direct me to a company that does have openings or perhaps an agency that places aircraft engineers. Gee, any other ideas you might have along these lines would really be appreciated. . . .

PD: Well, I understand Martin Aviation is hiring. But if you strike out there you can call Paul Delt and Associates in Los Angeles. That's where we get a good many of our referrals.

JIM: Terrific. Thanks. I really appreciate you taking the time to help me this morning. I know you're really busy. And Rachel?

PD: Yes?

JIM: May I leave you my name and number, or send you a packet on myself for your files just in case something opens up?

PD: Sure, send us your information. We hire from time to time.

JIM: Great. One more thing: I'd like to add your name and number to my personal networking sourcebook. Would that be okay with you?

PD: Well, sure, I guess so.

JIM: Good. You just seem like someone I could call occasionally for ideas or leads.

PD: Sure, no problem. Best of luck in your job search.

JIM: Hey, thanks. I appreciate the kind words and your information. You've been really helpful.

PD: Sure, bye.

JIM: Bye. Have a great day and I hope we talk soon.

As you can see, Jim Jones was much more friendly and personable in this scene. He asked the person's name, and called her by it; made his requests short and to the point; asked to send information to stay in touch with her; was courteous and upbeat and, most of all, accomplished the goal of making a new networking connection while getting two others. Notice how the conversation honored the basic improv rules we talked about earlier. After a dozen calls like this a day, you can only imagine how many leads you might have by day's end.

So remember to be friendly. Keep your comments short, concise, easy to assimilate and polite. Make sure you've reached the goal you set out to accomplish. And keep that filing system intact and current! This is when its importance becomes even more relevant. Pause briefly to make those notes in the comment section.

ACTING ON A REFERRAL

Let's move on to the second category: calling on someone you've been referred to by someone else. Let's say Jim Jones has decided to follow up on Rachel Smith's lead and call Paul Delt at the headhunter company she referred to. This, too, will be an out-of-the-blue call, but now he has a name to use, which takes some of the tension out of the unknown.

TAKE ONE:
WOMAN: Paul Delt and Associates.
JIM: Paul Delt, please.
WOMAN: May I tell him who's calling?
JIM: Jim Jones.
  (She connects Jim.)
DELT: Paul Delt.
JIM: Hi, this is Jim Jones and I'm looking for a job.
DELT: Oh, uh-huh. . . .
JIM: Well, I was wondering—do you know any companies that are hiring?
DELT: Hiring? Gee, you really caught me at a bad time. I'm really busy. . . .
JIM: (Defensive) I'm sorry . . . I was just. . . .

DELT: Sorry. Listen, I'd really like to talk to you but I have a meeting in ten minutes. Send us a resume or something.
JIM: But, uh . . . okay.
  (Dial tone)

In this scene Jim Jones never even thanked the woman who answered the phone. Heck, she may become the company president next week! Also, Jim is vague in his presentation, and he hasn't created any good vibes, either. In fact, he not only lost Delt's interest early on; he slightly irritated him. So much for rapport. Even worse, I can almost guarantee that if Delt has a good memory and receives Jim's resume in the mail, he will throw it away. A good impression was not made. To have gotten this scene off to a strong start, Jim should have mentioned Rachel's name and used the tips in the public relations chapter. Introducing himself, all Jim could do is talk about himself and his needs. "I'm looking for a job"—not a very bright thing to say. Everyone calling Delt's agency is obviously looking for a job. Let's run this piece again from Delt's entrance.

TAKE TWO:
DELT: Paul Delt.
JIM: Hi, Mr. Delt, this is Jim Jones calling. Rachel from Boeing suggested I give you a call.
DELT: Oh, yeah. Rachel. How is she?
JIM: Terrific. Really a neat lady. She took the time to help me, and we'd just met.
DELT: Yeah, Rachel's like that. Once she helped me throw a baby shower for my secretary; I didn't know what in the world I was doing.
JIM: (Laughing) You know, I got that mothering sense about her, too. She just seemed like the kind of person who could take care of anything, anytime.

DELT: Oh, and there was this other time, when. . . .

(Jim and Delt banter about Rachel. Delt shares more stories; Jim keeps reacting and responding. He certainly didn't expect this, but stays in a be-here-now mode.) A few minutes later:

JIM: Well, I hope I get to know her better, she sounds really fun and certainly someone I'd like to have in my corner.

DELT: Yeah, she's great. So what can I do for you Jim?

JIM: Well, I'm an aircraft engineer and looking for work in that industry. I've got great credentials. May I set up a time to meet with you?

DELT: I don't really have anything right now, but let's get together next week, anyway. You sound like a promising candidate. I'd like to meet you just in case something comes up.

JIM: I know how busy you must be, and I so appreciate your time to do that, Mr. Delt. Really appreciate it. . . .

DELT: Call me Paul.

JIM: Oh, OK, Paul. I really appreciate the opportunity. Shall I send my resume package to you ahead of time, or would you prefer I bring it with me?

DELT: Go ahead and send it. I'll pass you back to Rosemary now. She schedules my calendar.

JIM: Terrific. I'll mail it today, Paul. And, I really look forward to meeting you.

DELT: Yes, me too. Later.

JIM: Bye.

As you can see, we have vibes galore. Because Jim was going with the direction of the conversation—discussing Rachel—every line served as another building block in the house of rapport. He also was in the modes of Serve and Support and React and Respond. Delt wanted to talk about his relationship with Rachel, and it provided a great opportunity for Jim to bond with Delt. By the time they had finished that digression, they had established rapport. That's all it usually takes to make a networking friend. As you can see in this case, Jim got an appointment with Delt. From that meeting, his goal is to get other names—people he can call on—who can help him thread his way to that engineering aircraft manufacturer job.

Remember Jim's assignments: to build rapport, get an appointment and collect other names of people who might help him in his job quest. In this scene he kept focused on those preset goals. Interestingly, it was Delt who made the gesture toward Jim for the meeting, but this is not uncommon when rapport exists. Delt knew Jim wanted to get a job or Jim wouldn't have called him. Delt also knew how important it would be to Jim to give him some of his valuable time.

Keep your eye on your goal to stay on course as you communicate. And always, *always*, establish rapport.

MORE TOOLS FOR YOUR TOOLBOX

Now that you've grasped some of the basic improv tenets that serve so well as guidelines to your own communications, I'd like to offer a few more. They are also designed to improve your communication skills and to make you more aware of your part as a good conversationalist. These tricks and secrets employed by the improv players always give them the edge when entering and engaging in any conversation.

Give and Take is a big issue with all improv players. There is never one star in any one scene; instead, dialogue moves back and forth equally. The players are careful not to step on each other's lines (dialogue). They engage in a verbal dance of sorts; sometimes one leads, the other follows and vice versa.

I want you to get familiar with **Economy of Dialogue**. In our work onstage, we are mandated to say only what is absolutely necessary. We can't get caught up in minutiae, become tangential or engage in expositional dialogue. Every word counts in our scenes, and since we usually have one to three minutes to present an entire scene, what we say has to be meaningful, pertinent to the piece and, in a nutshell, short and sweet but substantial. Improv players were into sound bites before anyone even coined the phrase. In our exchanges with others, especially in the workplace, we need to realize that everyone is busy, everyone has other things on their mind and they don't have time for us to think out loud (which many of us tend to do). Besides, when we're concise and to the point, we keep people's attention and are more interesting to listen to.

One more basic improv rule for your communication notebook is called **Creating Into Certainty**. It means just what it says. Rather than conversing in ambiguities, we speak in specifics. We can't spend the first few minutes of a scene trying to find out what the other is thinking or where the other is going with the scene; if we did, this is what it might sound like (which is not much different from many everyday scenes):

PERSON #1: Do you want to go there?
PERSON #2: Should we take him with us?

"What the heck are they talking about?" you might ask. Well, so would anybody else. Now,

if you were an improv player you could banter nonsensically for a good minute before there was any indication of what someone was talking about. That would be a sin, because we have so little time onstage to present a complete piece of work. Let's take another pass at those opening lines:

PERSON #1: Do you want to go to the store?
PERSON #2: Should we take Rover with us?

Creating Into Certainty allows the actors and audience to know immediately what is being talked about. You want to be conscious of your dialogue in the same manner. Be direct, clear and to the point.

Packing these three rules in your communication toolbox is a must. Combined with the others we covered, they truly give you the edge when talking to, and with, others.

FACE TO FACE

Let's take a look at a couple more before-and-after conversations. Both fall into our third category: someone you know only slightly. For the fun of it, let's first look in on that meeting between Delt and Jim as they get together:

TAKE ONE:
(Paul Delt greets Jim Jones in Delt's office.)
JIM: I brought another thing if you need one.
DELT: Uh, what? (No response from Jim) Well, how are—
JIM: Well, if you don't have any companies who are looking for someone with my abilities, as you said on the phone, I was hoping you might know someone who is.
DELT: (Uncomfortable and almost feeling embarrassed) Well, there are a few companies you might try sending your resume to. They

are . . . (he reels them off but Jim isn't taking notes).

JIM: Oh, thanks.

DELT: Sure.

JIM: Any other suggestions? I mean—

DELT: Not really. Say, I hate to cut this short but I have a meeting to go to.

JIM: You mean our meeting is over? I was hoping . . . well, when you said you'd meet with me I was looking forward to . . . what I mean to say is I was thinking that maybe you might . . . well . . . I don't want to impose but. . . .

DELT: I really have to get going now. (He stands and gestures toward the door.) I'll be in touch if I have any other ideas for you.

JIM: (Showing his disappointment) Oh. Thanks for the time.

What a mess. What's especially sad is that I've heard people do just this. They are so intent in getting what they want, or they are mentally unprepared—feeling awkward and showing their lack of self-confidence and poise—that they have made a feeble impression. Poor Jim has no clue how to maximize his "moment" with Delt or how to establish rapport. He was vague. He cut Delt off and showed little strength. And he violated the idea of Economy of Dialogue when he began to explain his feelings about the meeting, or try to. If we go back over the Beginning, Middle and End theory as well as Serve and Support, we see that Jim really doesn't score well. Being in the moment came and went, and React and Respond was nonexistent. Of course we have plenty of Refusal and Denial, too.

Let's take that scene from the top again, and see how much more effectively it could have been performed.

TAKE TWO:

(Delt's office. Jones enters.)

JIM: (Extending his hand for a hearty shake. Good eye contact) So good to meet you in person, Paul. And thanks for taking the time to meet with me.

DELT: My pleasure. Please have a seat.

JIM: Thanks. (Reaches in his notebook) Say, I happen to have another resume if you need one, and I also brought along some letters of reference if you'd like them.

DELT: Oh, thanks. (Reaches for them) I'll keep them in your file. (Pause) So, you're an engineer?

JIM: Yes, I am. I've been in the business for ten years now and just love it. I'm looking for something in the aircraft industry—the manufacturing end. Research and development or design. I'd like to find a company that has growth potential, good benefits and a team atmosphere.

DELT: Ah, I've got just the company—Jason Aircraft—but unfortunately they're not hiring right now. Maybe in a few months I could place you.

JIM: Oh, thanks. That's sounds promising. For now, however, I'd like to keep looking.

DELT: Yes, by all means. You should.

JIM: With that in mind, would you happen to know anyone I could contact who might know of any immediate openings? Or at least some opportunities I could check out?

DELT: Sure. (Grabs a piece of paper) I'm one step ahead of you. Here are two leads. Jerry Harcroft is an old buddy of mine, and he seems to know everyone in the aircraft and transportation field. My other pal, Don Mathey, used to be at Boeing and seems to know everybody who's anybody in the biz.

JIM: Oh, great. That's really helpful. I'll follow

up on these immediately. May I tell them you referred me?

DELT: By all means.

JIM: (Senses the meeting is over) Well, I know you've got lots to do so I won't keep you. (Looks toward Delt's desk and notices lots of soccer memorabilia. Thinks fast on his feet) You know, a college buddy of mine just printed the first issue of *Soccer Today*. I'll drop a copy in the mail to you. In fact, I know he's looking for guest columnists, maybe you. . . .

(They continue chatting about the magazine—Jim is building a bunch of rapport—then they say good-bye.)

JIM: Again, Paul, thanks a million.

DELT: No problem. Keep in touch. Let me know if you have any luck with my friends.

JIM: Hey, I will. And I'll call from time to time, if that's okay, to see if any requests have come your way for someone like me.

DELT: Cool.

As you can see, we have a warmer, more positive exchange between the two. Jim was respectful, attentive and appropriate. He took advantage of the meeting by getting more contacts, so it didn't matter if Delt didn't have any clients who could use him at the time. It also gave Jim a chance to make a good impression. You can be sure that when Jim goes home, he's going to write "crazy about soccer" in the comments column in his journal. That will cue him to send his friend's magazine and look for other opportunities to send Delt soccer-related items. The result: Jim gets to build on their relationship. It's impossible for Delt not to get attached to Jim. If Jim keeps this relationship alive—he only has to contact Delt every few months to make that happen—he will have a networking source

for life. Also, notice how nicely Jim played within the improv guidelines. All this took one phone call and one meeting. Think what you can do following in Jim's footsteps!

Let's look at another scene. First, we'll see what common mistakes can be made when meeting a new contact for the first time, then we'll critique what elements could have made that get-together more meaningful.

(Interior of office at the rear of a florist's shop. A woman, Mrs. Sardoff, is seated behind her desk, as a young lady, Martha Sarcher, enters.)

MARTHA: Gee, it's really cold in here.

MRS. SARDOFF: Oh, yes, sorry. We have to keep it that way. For the flowers and all.

MARTHA: Oh. (Embarrassed) I didn't know that.

MRS. SARDOFF: Did you bring a resume with you?

MARTHA: Well, no. I sent one like you asked when we talked.

MRS. SARDOFF: I'm not sure where I put it. Things are kind of messy here . . . (shuffling papers on her desk).

MARTHA: Well, I'm really creative, like it says in my resume, and I'm looking for contacts.

MRS. SARDOFF: In what field? What are your areas of interest?

MARTHA: Well in any field that has to do with decor, like the floral industry, interior design—like that.

MRS. SARDOFF: Well, I have an opening for a salesclerk if that's of interest.

MARTHA: Yeah, I guess. (Long pause) But, um. . . . (Lost for words)

MRS. SARDOFF: What's the job like?

MARTHA: Yeah. What kinds of things would I do?

(Mrs. Sardoff goes on to tell her about the job duties. She says she is still interviewing others for the position, and will contact her within a few days regarding her decision. Martha exits looking confused.)

From the outset of Martha's entrance she began to deny Mrs. Sardoff, albeit very subtly, by commenting on the temperature in the room. Unknowingly, she took one step further when she said she already sent a resume and didn't have another with her. She put Mrs. Sardoff in an awkward position—invalidated her, in effect. Since Martha had little regard for the Serve and Support and React and Respond rules of improvised conversation, the whole scene was out of balance.

Had she been in the moment, Martha would have been more attuned to what Mrs. Sardoff was trying to convey. For instance, Mrs. Sardoff was a bit embarrassed by having misplaced Martha's resume. Martha could have been sympathetic or expressed her understanding by saying something like, "Oh, no problem, I lose things all the time—you should see my desk!" Or, better yet, she could have been more prepared and had another resume with her to avoid that uncomfortable moment.

Also, when Mrs. Sardoff was trying to glean from Martha her areas of interest, Martha did not create into certainty all that well. She was not terribly specific. When asked about her areas of interest, she could have said, "I would very much like to be in a job that allows me to express my creativity through design. That could be anything from a job as a floral arranger to someone who decorates homes and offices." That would have given Mrs. Sardoff a clearer signal.

Finally, Martha didn't show much interest or enthusiasm when it came to the sales position. Whether she wanted that job or not, she could have been more responsive to Mrs. Sardoff's statement. At the end of the conversation, Martha almost lost her composure; since she was not in the moment or reacting and responding to the last thing said, there were awkward pauses. The flow of conversation was interrupted. She should have said "Oh, a salesclerk. Sounds intriguing. Can you tell me more about it?" As you can see, there was no real end to this conversation. Martha left in a confused state, and nothing was said to indicate she would like to apply for the salesclerk position. Mrs. Sardoff was no doubt underwhelmed, because Martha didn't come across as someone who was too together.

LONG TIME NO TALK

We all neglect our associates and colleagues because we're all too busy. The relationships with these people are like plants, however; we have to take the time to "water" them to keep them alive and growing. But what happens if you just can't stay in touch as often as you'd like, and suddenly you need to call and ask a favor, like "who do you know that? . . ."

Well, you have several choices: You can apologize right before you make your request, you can be direct and tell them they can pull the same thing on you any time they want or you can open your remarks with a humorous icebreaker (my favorite). Whenever I call someone I haven't spoken to in a while, and we both know I'm calling because I want something, I say one of the following:

- "I'm calling because I need _____ . Actually, that's just an excuse, I'm calling because I've really missed you." (They say, "Yeah, right.")
- "Hey, how come you're not returning my phone calls?" (They usually say, "Get outta here. Where have you been?")

- "Would you mind loaning me $25,000? Well, never mind, that's a lot to ask. How about another favor, then. Say, who do you know that? . . ."
- "How come you never call me?" (They usually say "*mee-e?*")
- When they pick up the phone I yell, "HELLLLLP!"

There are a number of ways to handle the awkwardness of calling someone you know but haven't talked to for some time because you need a networking source from them. Don't be too reticent to make that call for help. First, realize one thing: It's okay to call out of the blue and ask a favor of someone you know because it usually makes the person feel good. We all like to feel needed.

Me? I don't mind someone calling to ask for a contact if they're respectful and take a minute to see how I am. The one thing I despise is when someone calls and just makes their need known, without even saying "How are you?" or saying it, but not meaning it. Don't forget with this group—people you know but haven't talked to for a long time—it's important that you stay in the rapport-building mode. The more rapport you build, the stronger the relationship becomes. Strong relationships can serve as your networking backbone and solidify your base over time.

I have one friend whom I probably talk to once every two years. When I do call I usually need something from her. Same with her when she calls me. We formed a solid bond twenty-seven years ago. The older you get, the more likely you, too, will develop such relationships. Cherish them. Remember, in business, it's always a numbers game; that includes accumulating relationships.

When you're in a situation where you have to

call people you haven't talked to for some time, my advice is that you throw out an icebreaker, whether it's humorous or not. Show some interest in *them*—always!

In lieu of humor, start such conversations by asking your contact about something in her life that was going on the last you spoke. I always keep my journal of contact information filled in because when I go to call someone I haven't talked to for several months or even a year, it will trigger a dialogue connector. This connector provides an opportunity to rekindle our relationship. Just last week I talked to three people I hadn't spoken to in more than a year. Here were my openers as they said hello:

1. "Bart, first question: Whatever happened to your son, the one who sprayed the dorm walls with grafitti?" We laughed. We talked. Then we did business.

2. "Thanks for taking my call. I really need your help." (I knew he was busy and got right to the point. He was grateful and I got what I needed).

3. "If I'm imposing by asking you the question I'm about to ask you, just tell me I'm rude, dammit, but don't deny me, I'm in network hell and you're the only one who can get me out." (She laughed and told me she was in hair hell; she'd gotten her coif hacked by a new hairdresser. I promised to let her borrow my favorite hat in trade for a couple of phone numbers and the right to drop her name. We verbally shook on the deal and did our business.)

Don't get so locked into your agenda that the first words out of your mouth are related to your request. When the person you're contacting answers the phone (or you see them in person) and hears your request—"Hi, Jane, this is Sandy. Say, I'm in need of a contact in the video editing business. I need someone who might want to donate their services for a charity event. Know anyone?"—where's the human connection? Where's the care-about-the-other-guy attitude? Where's the rapport?

You need great communication skills to build rapport and that just might include chewing the fat—sometimes more than just a layer or two.

Whatever the conversation takes to make it work, do it. Go with whatever is happening right there, right then. Let the scene have a life of its own. Forget control. Use all the improv comedy ground rules to bolster your technique. You can't possibly fail. Much to the contrary, you will always get what you're after, especially when it comes to communicating with this diverse group.

YOU AGAIN?

I don't know about you, but sometimes I find it difficult to ask people I know really well for something. I actually find it easier to approach a stranger. Whether you find it easier or harder, as with the preceding groups, the same rules apply for the people we talk to all the time.

First, remember your improv lessons. You want to be polite, show interest in the other person and take time for personal conversation. Don't take advantage of their goodwill just because you know each other well. Don't forget the rule in chapter nine: For every one thing a person does for you (a contact name, for instance), give two things back. Yes, even for friends and family—the people whose help we perceive as a "given." They can be little things like a thank-you note and an interesting article, a follow-up thank-you voice mail message or a fax of a funny cartoon. It's easy to forget, pass over or take advantage of those closest to you, but don't treat the familiar people any differently from those you're trying to impress.

The one marked difference between this cat-

egory and all the others is that the dialogue can be more relaxed and casual. After all, the people we talk to all the time are most probably family, friends or buddy-type business associates with whom we are less guarded and more trusting and comfortable.

For example, I wouldn't call my sister and say: "Oh, hello Heather, this is Cherie and I was wondering if I could take a minute of your time to ask whether or not you know anyone on staff at *Good Morning America*." She would probably burst out laughing. That is just not our format for conversing. But I know people who put on their business-suit demeanor with close ones just because they're asking a business question or favor. With my sister, the conversation would go something like this: "Babe, tell me you have a contact at *Good Morning America* so I don't have to jump out the window." She might say "no" (so I would press her to find me one) but the terms of our relating would be the same if we were talking about family stuff. So the message is, don't change personality or communication style just because you're in need of something business oriented.

What you want to guard against, however, is leaning too hard on those you know well; every one of us resents feeling used. I have a friend in film production who makes entries in a diary every day. His notes provide snippets of whom he called, when and for what reason. He swears by this because he calls so many people every day that after a couple of weeks, he can't keep track of things. He also told me he always makes a note of what he did for them (those little return favors that we talked about in the chapter seven), so he's able to stay on top of his game. He confided that he looks back through his journal entries every month to "check the score." I always scribble notes when I'm on the phone, even if it's with my sister, because I also talk to many people throughout the day, and I tend to get on overload and become forgetful. I don't want to ever take advantage of anyone; I'm trying to build relationships that last.

TALK IS CHEAP

Begin your tasks relating to this chapter's lessons by making a record of some conversations you've had with potential networking leads. Ask yourself: Were you polite? To the point? Clear on what you wanted and needed? Appreciative? Did you call the person by name? Did you leave the person feeling good about you? Your checklist should be your starting point as you build your style as a communication artisan. Without good communication skills you're like a ballet dancer without a slipper; it's a little hard to get around.

Always be clear and articulate. Realize the other person is not inside your head; when you convey your ideas and needs, make them easy to understand. Also, be a good listener. Listening is a more active part of conversations than you may have thought. Just because the other person is doing most of the talking doesn't mean you're not involved in conversation. Listen to everything, including a person's subtext (what is unsaid).

Positive energy is irresistible when you present yourself as upbeat, people are more receptive to your ideas and ready to converse with you. I can't stress this enough: Be sincere and polite at all times. Have a genuine attitude in all your dealings; people can tell when you feign interest or are the slightest bit rude.

Review

Let's recap the highlights of communication skills that build rapport:

1. Every scene—piece of communication—will be different, so be prepared for the unexpected.
2. Everyone you come across will have different backgrounds, likes, dislikes and moods. Pay close attention to where they're coming from in their communication so you can play off them.
3. Every scene should have a beginning, middle and an end.
4. Serve and support. Think of them first, you second.
5. React and respond. Address the last thing said or last idea held. Add information to keep the conversation moving forward and evolving productively.
6. Be here now. Stay in the moment—always.
7. Don't refuse or deny. To refuse is to ignore something someone says; to deny is to change or undercut what they say.
8. Give and take. Don't step on people's "lines." Think equality in arriving at a balance of dialogue.
9. Economy of dialogue. Keep your dialogue concise and to the point; don't get expositional and don't digress.
10. Create into certainty. Speak in specifics, not generalities. Keep your comments and responses clear and easy to assimilate.
11. Converse with intelligence, courtesy, poise, presence and when appropriate, a sense of humor.
12. Be clear, articulate, upbeat and positive, sincere and polite at all times. Be a good listener.
13. Your job is to build rapport and get contacts and leads. Keep your eye on that goal in all your communication.
14. Use an icebreaker to rekindle the relationship with people you don't talk to frequently.

Don't forget to start the conversation with dialogue that shows interest in them. Use a connector (where did you leave off with them when you last spoke). Take good care of them. Check your notes to see if you are giving back more than you get.

15. Don't abuse your contacts.

16. Let each scene have a life of its own. Forget control. Go with the flow.

17. Don't change style or personality just because it's business.

ASSIGNMENTS

The following are a few assignments to rehearse your new communication techniques:

1. Pick a fifteen-minute time period each day and find someone with whom to converse. As you do, put into play all the things we've just covered. If you have to concentrate on a few ideas at a time—i.e., beginning, middle and end; creating into certainty; be here now—that's okay. Soon you'll incorporate these new techniques until they blend beautifully to make you a killer communicator. You can do this role-play with a friend or family member. Maybe even tape the sessions and critique them. There's nothing more educational than watching or hearing yourself in action.

2. Just for fun, write down a couple of mock conversations you think you might have as you come upon a contact you've never met before. Do the same for people you're networking with for the first time and people you talk to infrequently. Writing these out (you get to play both parts) helps you get a good handle on what sounds good and what doesn't. It may seem like a slow process at first, but it's well worth the time. It will feel like you're conversing in slow motion as you write your script. The result: great reinforcement of all you've learned in this chapter.

3. Build rapport with at least three strangers each day. They can be next to you in the elevator, the person you never bothered to strike up a conversation with, like the teenager who checks your groceries or the neighbor you've only said hello to. Establish relationships with people you've never met before or have only said hello to on occasion.

You'd be surprised how many new friends and contacts you're going to make through this exercise. It's great rehearsal for what you'll come up against on the job.

4. During one conversation each day, do nothing but listen to every word the other person is saying. By the end of the conversation, see if you heard things you would normally have tuned out. Make note of how many times your mind might drift or go back to focusing on yourself.

5. Keep an ongoing record of how many new relationships you've built in the homework process. They won't necessarily be relationships you can network with; nonetheless, keeping track of random encounters and the new acquaintances you make will boost your confidence in your ability to communicate well and understand the value of the rapport-building process.

chapter ten

The Do's and Don'ts of Interviewing

nterviewing requires coming together with other people; every time you come in contact with another human being, you create another opportunity for networking. For instance, you may not land a particular job but the person who interviewed you may refer you to someone else more likely to hire you. Whenever you deal with people, you increase your odds for making new connections, thus, additional networking possibilities.

As you interview and make new contacts, presenting yourself well is one more way to build rapport and forge strong, positive connections.

Knowing how to present yourself well to a potential employer is paramount. It's critical that you say and do all the right things during your interviews. The people with whom you interview will make decisions based on your responses, inquiries, presentation and attitude—in general, how you come across. They will also judge you on personal appearance and demeanor.

You've worked hard to get to this stage, so you want every interview to result in a job offer.

THINKING AHEAD

You need to consider some basics before you leave for the interview. Think ahead to possible obstacles that could prevent you from being on time or getting distracted by the unexpected. For instance, do you know how much time it will take to get there? Did you anticipate road construction or other possible delays? Is your interview during peak traffic times? Will weather be a factor? Is parking a problem? Will you need money to get out of the parking lot? If so, how much? Do you know where the entrance is and the route to the office where your interview is to be held? Will you need time to sign in with the receptionist? Will you need an umbrella? Will you need to use the restroom to freshen up or check your appearance one last time? All this leads to one important aspect of the interviewing process: *You will need to be on time.* If you're late, it will be hard to gain the respect from your prospective employer. No one can accept tardiness. It screams "I am not really professional." If there is an accident or other legitimate reason for being late, stop and call. It's better to prepare the prospective employer for lateness than to show up and offer an apology. Calling ahead sounds more believable.

Plan to show up early. When you're early you can always relax a minute and get centered before the interview. You also can get a feel for the environment. You want to be calm, collected and confident when you walk in for the interview. That may not happen if you're flying through the door breathlessly asking to see Ms. So-and-So.

REHEARSE FIRST

Preparing for an interview is like preparing for a theatrical performance—you need to rehearse. In addition to practicing possible dialogue, rehearse the way you carry yourself, sit and use your voice, facial expression and body language—all of which I refer to as "presence." The minute you walk into someone's office, your audience will form a definite and lasting opinion, much of it subconscious. Come across as professional and confident. Be mindful of how you "take the stage" and perform.

While you're in the practice mode, make a list of possible answers to frequently asked questions, so you will be ready with appropriate responses. Such questions may include:
- What is your experience?
- What are your goals?
- Why do you want this particular job?
- What can you bring to the position?
- Why should we hire you?
- Why are you leaving, or why did you leave, your last position?

Candidates tend to get long-winded, so make a punch list of highlights to answer each of these questions and choose your words carefully. Be succinct.

WARMING UP

As crazy as it may sound, warm up before any interview. Warming up includes vocalizing in the car on your way over, getting your breathing intact and working on your energy level. You're no different than an actor going on an audition or getting ready for a performance, but your performance will be at the job interview. Many actors have only a few minutes to read the audition scripts they're given and impress a producer or casting director. They don't have the luxury of warming up on the spot; instead they do so beforehand, so when it's their time to audition, the first words out of their mouths sound smooth and powerful. You, too, may have only a few minutes with a decision maker, so you don't want to be getting your performance level together *during* the interview.

Your voice, energy level and poise will tell your interviewer a great deal about you the minute you deliver your first words. It is at that early stage that some bosses form a strong opinion; some even make their decision.

BREATHE IN, SPEAK OUT

It could be fatal to appear nervous during that important interview, and your voice is one thing that will give you away if you are. A confident voice radiates poise but can't be had with labored or shallow breathing. Many people give their nervousness away because they can't seem to regulate their breathing. Erratic breathing doesn't project confidence, nor does it provide you with the best vocal production (sound of your voice). Learning to breathe diaphragmatically is essential to feeling and sounding good. It's what all actors and singers use to boost the power in their voices and get more resonance and range in their sound. If you're one of those monotone types, or if your voice becomes strident or strained when you get uncomfortable, you must learn to breathe properly. Remember good breathing has everything to do with "cotton mouth" syndrome, another indicator that you're scared or uncomfortable. When your breathing becomes more shallow it interrupts the regular flow of some bodily secretions, your saliva glands being one of them. However, if your breathing is even and regulated, all bodily systems will respond normally. Irregular breathing also causes other problems, like hyperventilation. The practice of proper breathing technique is essential. You'll find exercises to help you develop these techniques on page 103.

FIRE UP AND BE ON

Just like actors you want to appear alert, ready and primed for your interview. Do what performers do and get fired up before you walk in the door. Talk out loud in the car with animation about some particular pet peeve or psyche yourself silently by repeating a host of positives like, "OK, it's the big one, I'm gonna knock 'em dead" or "I am a terrific candidate for this job, oh yes I am!" My friend, the late comedian Phil Hartman, used to say, "If you believe it, *they'll* believe it."

You want to feel energized and positive when you shake that other person's hand. That's the place you want to get to when you "take the stage." This is not to say you're going to be manic, it simply means you're going to be dynamic as you begin to converse.

Energy is a funny thing, especially positive energy. If we lack it, we don't connect with oth-

ers; if it's present, we are impossible to resist. So make sure you fire up like actors and athletes before a big event (and to them every event is big—it should be to you, too). For some energy-boosting exercises, see page 104.

ENUNCIATE

One more aspect of finishing off your sense of presence is diction.

I am tyrannical with my students when they don't cleanly pronounce every syllable of every word. Poor diction says we are unprofessional, so learning to speak impeccably is terribly important. People who enunciate are always trusted by others on a subconscious level. Besides, no one interviewing you should have to strain to understand what you're saying. Nearly every job requires good verbal skills, which includes the way we pronounce our words. See page 104 for a few tips on better elocution.

BODY LANGUAGE SPEAKS VOLUMES

There are tons of books on body language, and you can read all of them. For now, I'm going to provide you with just a handful of recommendations that will assure not only your best foot goes forward, but also the rest of you as well.

Never look at the floor when you make your entrance. Looking down conveys that you feel inferior or inadequate, even if you look downward for a fleeting second. If you're pensive as you pause to answer a question, look upward rather than down. The rest of the time keep your head and eyes level.

Always sit up straight. Never slouch or slink down in your chair; both of these body language messages tell a loud story. Slouching doesn't speak well of your self-esteem, and slinking says you're unprofessional and immature. You don't need to sit stiffly, just straighten your shoulders. The easiest way to do this is to sit at the edge of the chair, which forces your spine to be erect, or to sit with your buttocks and back pressed against the back of the chair. These two positions assure good posture. Remember: How you carry yourself tells people how you feel about yourself. You want them to sense your confidence.

Keep eye contact as much as possible without making the other person uncomfortable. If you have a hard time keeping eye contact because you feel self-conscious or shy, just look at the bridge of the other person's nose. It will appear that you're looking in their eyes. This tactic gives you time to collect yourself until you can look them straight in the eye again. It also allows you to stay connected.

Don't fidget with your pen, purse or briefcase; wring your hands; pull on your clothing; itch your nose or play with your hair. Keep your hands off your face. Stay calm, poised and still. Animate slightly with your facial features, let your hands naturally follow your dialogue, and keep both hands visible at all times (seeing both hands is a trust issue). Watch the note taking. Only write something down if it's appropriate, like the name of this person's supervisor who will interview you next. I dislike when job candidates take notes as I'm talking to them; it makes me feel like I'm on trial in some way. It's an imperious gesture that makes your potential boss feel like *you're* interviewing him. Think "minimal."

Keep both feet on the floor; if you cross your legs, do so gracefully. Watch crossing your arms in front of you (it says "keep away"), and don't forget to smile occasionally. Oftentimes when we're in an interview our facial muscles tend to tense. We look like we're ready for war rather than work. Also, keep that head level; tilting it even slightly backward indicates arrogance.

Leave your nervous tics—like pulling the knot on your tie or fiddling with your earrings—at home or in the car. A job interview is no place to display them. It tells the other person you are neurotic and uncomfortable. Remember what I said about your audience mirroring you. I almost witnessed a self-strangulation with a woman who couldn't let go of the pearls around her neck.

Never chew gum, and always carry tissues or a hankie with you in case you sneeze. *Never* blow your nose in an interview.

Let people know you are solid, professional and have style and poise. Your body will tell that story if you let it speak positively for you. Don't forget how powerful these subtle signals can be—for good or bad.

DRESS FOR SUCCESS

There are hundreds of books on what to wear to an interview, but it's really quite simple: Wear your very best outfit, the one you save for those "special occasions." How you look tells the prospective employer a great deal about you. It's the first thing I notice (because I love clothes) when a job candidate enters my office.

A smart suit that is subtle and tasteful will always be the right choice. Most experts I spoke to said dark or muted colors such as blue, black, gray, brown or dark olive are best for both men and women. Human resource consultant Carol Cranfield, who places executives with Fortune 500 companies across the country, told me that corporate America still wants women to dress in skirts and dresses; pantsuits don't appeal to many decision makers. "They have a hard time seeing women as feminine when they're wearing pants," Carol said. But others said women wearing pants projected strength and a business mentality.

I say wear whatever is "you"—as long as it errs on the conservative side. Something simple and tailored always works, and you can never go wrong with a white shirt or blouse. Make sure your clothes fit you well; nothing too big and baggy and definitely nothing too tight. Pastels, such as blue, green, yellow and pink, are good to wear underneath that suit (I must say nothing appeals more to me than a man in a pink oxford shirt). Anything too loud, plaid, striped or tweed can be a problem. Tone down and go for something more understated.

Make certain your clothes are well pressed and clean. I don't want to show any gender bias, but I see more men than women with wrinkled clothes. If you're not good with the iron, invest in dry cleaning. By the way, a little starch in that cotton shirt looks full pro. Socks are a big thing. Make sure they don't upstage your look; they are meant to accent your wardrobe, not overtake it.

Your shoes should be well polished and never show signs of wear. Jewelry should be worn as it's intended—an accent and barely noticeable. Your hose should be flesh-colored or colored opaques that match your suit. Only wear a hint of perfume or cologne; nothing is more irritating than when someone leaves your office and his strong scent remains. It's an unconscious intrusion into someone's space.

Make certain your breath is fresh (the biggest turn-off in the world is bad breath) and women, wear makeup with care. Most appointments are during the day so you only need light, soft makeup. Overly made-up women turn everybody off. I'll never forget a woman I interviewed who was qualified for the spot, but whose face looked like it was going to jump off itself and across the desk at me. You could have frosted a five-layer cake with what she was wearing. I was too scared to think about hiring her. The person interviewing you shouldn't be aware of your makeup; they should only notice what nice features you have. Makeup is meant to bring out and distinguish what you have—not to overemphasize.

You are what you wear; that's how people perceive you. If you dress professionally and businesslike, that will be the first impression you make. If your interviewer is turned off by what you're wearing, and that's their initial take on you, you'll need to spend the rest of the interview trying to score extra points to get them to forgive your appearance and focus on your credentials and talent. Your clothes should enhance your overall appeal, not detract from it. As a final act, take another look in the mirror from all angles. Make sure your slip isn't showing, you don't have a visible panty line, your cuffs are turned properly, your belt goes through all the loops and your coat pleats aren't folded under your coattail or lining (a place that's hard to see). A rear view, side view and up-and-down glance are always the last assessments you should make before heading out the door.

IT'S THEIR SHOW

Many people are so eager to please and impress and share how wonderful they are, they barge into the interview with a zeal that is overwhelming. It comes across as though they are trying to control the conversation. They have so much they want that prospective employer to know that they dominate the interview. You should go on every appointment with the mind-set that it's their show and you will simply react and respond to their questions. You will play off of them, listen well and respond to the last thing said and last idea held. Nothing is more annoying to the interviewer than to be interrupted by the candidate who wedges his own thoughts and agenda into the conversation. The interviewer should always be left in charge. If the person wants you to tell your life story, she'll invite you to do so. Be respectful and perceptive, and follow their lead. They are the boss. Each potential employer has a specific point of view on what she is looking for in the person she will hire; her line of questioning will reflect that. Be sure not to appear presumptuous by asserting yourself verbally.

The person interviewing you will want you to be concise and to the point with your answers, as I mentioned in chapter nine. Make sure you don't get tangential or verbose as you reply. If the person hiring you is your potential boss, he will note how well you follow direction and acquiesce to his needs and requests. No matter how many people meet with you prior, you will ultimately have to interview with the person who will be your immediate supervisor. Let them know indirectly that you're the kind of person who would be confident and professional, while also subordinate to them.

I base my hiring decisions primarily on attitude. If it's apparent to me in the initial interview that a person is competitive with me or that they're trying to override my authority in even the slightest way, he's out the door. I don't want a total "yes" person, but I do want respect. I deserve it. I'm the one in charge; I'm doing the hiring and I write the checks. So, as my grandfather used to say, "Don't be cheeky darlin'." Cheeky is the softer side of arrogant. No one likes it, and it has no place in an interview.

Again, presentation is key. You must be prepared to show everything that's important—samples, letters of recommendation and so forth. Have anything they may ask you for handy (I know someone who walks in with a small day planner but leaves everything in the car, in case) because you never know from interview to interview what will be asked of you. You can always take a moment or two at the end of the interview to say something like, "Before I go, there are a couple of things I would like to tell you about myself that we've not yet covered. . . ."

IF YOU CAN'T SAY ANYTHING NICE, DON'T SAY IT AT ALL

One of the most common mistakes job candidates make is that they share a negative experience or feeling about a former employer, coworker or company. It is almost instant death to ever deride someone or something during a job interview. You may have valid reasons for why you left your last job or why you're looking for a new job, but tell your shrink or best friend, not your prospective employer. No one likes a tattletale nor do they want to hear negatives. This is not to say you can't diplomatically allude to your reason for leaving a job; just do it with class.

For example, I interviewed two guys one afternoon. The first told me a few horror stories about his former boss in lurid detail. Though the candidate that followed him also seemed displeased with his former boss, he chose to answer my question, "Why are you leaving your job?" with, "I just don't feel my values and those of the company with which I'm currently working are aligned. It's been a wonderful experience and I'm most appreciative for it, but it's time for me to move on." The other gentleman, whom I really liked, incidentally, said in response to the same question: "My boss thinks he's Donald Trump; what an egomaniac. And besides, quite frankly, I do like to play squash at least three times a week after work, and he can't handle that." He never should have told me either of those things; it put me on guard.

Most employers think if you say something bad about your last boss, you are bound to do the same with them. Though some supervisors are impossible, you should never bad-mouth them to anyone in the workplace. It shows you can be the bigger person. It also demonstrates that you can handle yourself no matter how many difficult people you run into. Believe me, there is no job in the world where someone in your work environment isn't somewhat trying at times. Your ability to field such problems says a lot to a would-be employer. I always pay great attention to the person I try to trick into telling me something I shouldn't know. All employers test their job candidates in different ways. Learning to steer clear of office politics goes beyond the office in which you're currently working; it spills over into your next job.

When you're leaving one job to go to another, there is often a negative reason for making such a departure and the interviewer knows that. If you share your woes, however, you might close the door on that job. So be careful what you say about the people you've worked for, and always take the high road. You can't make a mistake that way.

WHAT EVERY EMPLOYER IS LOOKING FOR

A number of employers, headhunters and employment-agency owners I surveyed revealed that what they are each looking for in a job candidate is similar across the board. The following list is a compilation of comments they made when asked what seemed to be most important in choosing a new employee:

1. Someone who can follow directions but who is also able to lead when necessary.
2. Someone who is accountable and takes responsibility for his or her work results.
3. Someone who is upbeat and positive; who will do whatever it takes to get the job done.
4. Someone who is creative and resourceful; who can think "outside the box."
5. Someone who is always a team player.
6. Someone who takes criticism well and lets it guide them positively.
7. Someone who makes the company "look good."
8. Someone who can be consistent under pressure.
9. Someone who genuinely cares about the growth and success of the company.
10. Someone who is self-motivated.
11. Someone who is confident and self-assured.
12. Someone who possesses a good sense of humor.

As you go about considering the "do's" of interviewing, keep this list in mind and let it guide your responses and comments.

Since I've itemized the top do's of interviewing, it's also worth passing along to you what this same group said relative to the "don'ts" of interviewing—or more directly, what their pet peeves were about job candidates and employees.

1. Someone who chronically blames job-related problems on the other guy.
2. Someone who is clearly out for themselves—always thinking "me first."
3. Someone who lacks maturity and professionalism.
4. Someone who has to be constantly directed as they go about job tasks.
5. Someone who overreacts to stress and who takes things personally.

6. Someone who gossips about people at work.
7. Someone who can't laugh at himself or herself.
8. Someone who displays traits of insecurity.
9. Someone who does not listen.
10. Someone who puts great emphasis on the paycheck and the benefits.
11. Someone who complains about anything and everything.
12. Someone who projects a negative image of the company.

With this list of grievances in mind, be careful what you say during that interview, whether it's for a job or just a friendly chat with a networking source. Leave your problems and dislikes at home. Let people know by your attitude that you are confident, capable and professional.

FOLLOW UP

One way to follow up a job interview with a great impression is to send a note after the interview. Be careful of a standard computer-generated letter. I prefer receiving a handwritten note from people who want a job (or network source) from me because it has a personal touch. You want to reinforce that positive impression, not take away from it, so be wary of the boilerplate "thanks for the interview" approach. I can smell those the minute I open one. It turns me off. If someone really wants the job I'm offering, I will know it by the way they follow-up.

To follow-up, feel free to telephone. As I mentioned earlier, it shows your interest in wanting the job. But be very careful not to call too soon, and don't badger them. Nothing is worse than when a job candidate calls me constantly to see whether or not I've made a decision. It makes you seem desperate, and you don't want to give that impression, even if it's the job you want so badly you'd crawl through glass in the desert to get it.

Show interest by calling, but don't be too persistent. Wait four to five days between follow-up calls if they leave you hanging. What's even better is to ask the interviewer when it would be a propitious time for you to check back. If after a few phone calls the person hasn't responded positively, let it go and move on to the next possibility.

THE FUNDAMENTAL WORKOUT

The following is a condensed recap of this chapter. Doing the exercises will maximize your success and comfort level in interviews.

These exercises will help you breathe properly, warm up your voice, improve your diction and build your energy level.

Breathing

1. Stand straight and tall with your shoulders back, chest out. This good posture opens up the area that houses your diaphragm (right above your stomach).

2. To learn how this muscle works, pretend you're repeatedly blowing out birthday candles on a cake. You should feel your upper midriff move in and out. Next, take a deep breath, press your hand against your diaphragm, and slowly let the air out through your mouth. When all the air is released (let it out completely), don't take a conscious breath; instead, drop your lower jaw and let the air rush in and fill your diaphragm (like opening a window and allowing air to come through). In doing this several times a day, you will retrain the way you breathe when you're speaking. This type of breathing will also make you feel more comfortable when you get nervous. Do several of these inhale/exhale breaths consecutively.

3. Another great breathing exercise for reeducating that diaphragm is to put your hand on your midriff and do any variation of "HAH! HAH! HAH! HAH! HAH!" You'll feel your diaphragm contract and release as you strengthen the muscle.

4. Take a diaphragmatic breath and begin talking, slowly releasing air from your diaphragm as you speak. Try to speak as long as possible before taking another breath. Any series of "H" words such as "Honolulu," "hospital" or "hallelujah," are great to practice with. Make certain the air is pushing the words forward and out of your mouth. You should be able to feel the force of the air behind the words. Believe it or not, many people try to speak on the inhale; this is what makes them sound breathless and feel uncomfortable.

Practice your breathing exercises every day so when you're suddenly under pressure, your proper breathing technique will take over (subconsciously) and keep you solid. More importantly, you will use all facets of your voice, making it sound fuller, richer and stronger.

Diction

These homework tasks will improve the way you say your words. No matter how proficient you think you may already be, do them anyway. They are great drills.

1. Put a wooden pencil between your teeth in the front where it's hard to hold, and bite down on it securely. Begin speaking, saying anything slowly and deliberately. Over-pronounce every syllable of every word. After about a minute, release the pencil but keep speaking. You will hear a marked difference in the clarity of your speech, especially your *d's*, *k's*, *r's* and *s's*. Do this exercise daily, without fail. After about

three weeks your diction should be much cleaner. Take time each day to listen to yourself talk. Do you sound better, more professional?

2. Tongue twisters are a remarkable way to improve diction. There are three I like very much. The first works your lips and helps loosen the front portion of your mouth. After several, your lips should tingle. Say "rubber baby buggy bumpers" fast and furious. It doesn't matter if you say it perfectly; what's more important is that you are working that part of your mouth strenuously.

Next, work on your tongue. It is a muscle you want to build and tone. Your tongue forms the sounds you make. Say "red leather, yellow leather" quickly for as long as you can. Be sure to pronounce the *d's* and *r's*.

To get the back of your throat in gear say, "unique New York" over and over until the muscles in your throat tighten.

There are many other diction exercises, but these are enough to provide great improvement. All of us need to constantly "workout" when it comes to diction.

Energy

Your display of personal energy tells your potential employer a great deal. No one likes a deadbeat, and if you're the least bit monotone, you'll turn that person off. These exercises will help you get fired up.

1. Sit still and rub your hands together as hard and quickly as you can. You will begin to feel heat. That tells you what you want to stay in touch with: that you are made up of energy. Rubbing your hands together stimulates a physical spark that should begin to ignite your mental energy.

2. Practice talking out loud in a safe environ-

ment, such as your living room or car, and express your strong feelings on any subject. This begins to stimulate mental energy. After a minute or two of blabbering, you should feel the mental "burn" and be ready and alert for whatever comes your way. When our mental energy is stimulated, we are spontaneous and mentally agile.

3. If you are able, engage in something physical like pacing, dancing or exercising. Any physical activity gets you going.

4. Describe something giant, like the world's largest pencil. Express this with overly animated features and gestures. This, too, creates a great deal of energy.

Don't forget: Energy is what puts us across to the person on the other side of the desk during that interview. Without energy, we cannot make that human connection. And we want to create a connection, because with it comes rapport.

Body Language

Most of the time we don't have to say a thing; our body language tells its own story. Videotape yourself in a mock interview, and see if you're sending out any counterproductive signals. The following are reminders for handling appropriate body language.

1. Sit up straight but not stiffly.

2. Don't look at the floor or look down; instead, look up if you break eye contact.

3. Make eye contact as much as you can without making the other person or yourself uncomfortable. If you lose your composure, look at the bridge of the other person's nose. If you're being interviewed by a group of people, stay on each person for at least five seconds the first time you make eye contact with them. It will allow you to bond with your interviewers. When you make eye contact again, you will have already established rapport and will feel more connected. Make sure you evenly dispense your eye contact around the room as you talk to your panel of interviewers. Don't play favorites.

4. Don't fidget, display nervous tics or blow your nose.

5. Keep both hands visible. It provides a message of trust.

6. Don't fold your arms in front of your chest or display any other body language that says you're not approachable.

7. Animate slightly with facial features, and let your hands naturally follow your dialogue.

What To Wear

We talked about always looking your best for every interview. The following are some pointers to keep in mind when you put your wardrobe together.

1. Wear your best suit in muted colors such as brown, gray, black, navy or dark olive.

2. Make sure your shirt or blouse is either white or pastel.

3. No heavy cologne or perfume.

4. No wrinkled clothes or clothes that don't fit properly.

5. Make sure your shoes are polished and don't show strains of wear.

6. Makeup, jewelry and hairstyles should be simple and understated. Too much of any one of these is not only distracting but presents a not-too-pretty picture. Guys, leave the earring at home; it still isn't all that accepted in corporate America.

Check yourself in the mirror for a thorough once-over. You can also videotape yourself from head to toe and stand back for a closer look. Do you like what you see?

YOUR INTERVIEW WORKSHEET

1. I want this particular job because:
   A) _____
   B) _____
   C) _____
   D) _____
   E) _____

2. I'm leaving (or have left) my last position because:
   A) _____
   B) _____
   C) _____
   D) _____
   E) _____

3. You should hire me for the following reasons:
   A) _____
   B) _____
   C) _____
   D) _____
   E) _____

4. What I can bring to the company that is different and/or positive:
   A) _____
   B) _____
   C) _____
   D) _____
   E) _____

5. The following experience qualifies me perfectly for the job:
   A) _____
   B) _____
   C) _____
   D) _____
   E) _____

6. Before I go, there's a few things I'd like you to know about me, such as:
   A) _____
   B) _____
   C) _____
   D) _____
   E) _____

Fine-Tune Your Rehearsal Technqiues

We talked earlier about practicing some of the things you might say to your prospective employer. The preceding worksheet is a list of questions I want you to be prepared to answer. As you formed and clarified your thoughts, you wrote your answers down. You now have a loose "script" from which to review and study right before that interview.

Following Up On the Follow-Through

Following up is an important part of the interview process. Let's review those guidelines:

1. Don't call too soon or too often. Don't call sooner than five days or not until the day after they said they would call you.

2. Send a personal note, whether it is computer generated or handwritten.

3. Don't badger or come across as desperate or needy in your follow-up efforts. No one wants to hire someone who isn't confident.

In all your interview activities, make sure you acknowledge it is "their show." Follow the interviewer's lead, be responsive and gracious, respectful and polite. Be alert and ready for whatever questions may come your way.

Listen, listen, listen. Be spontaneous and self-assured.

chapter eleven

Networking for First-Timers, Second-Timers and Old-Timers

If you're a professional well ensconced in the business community, networking will no doubt be easier. You're right where you need to be to make contacts and utilize them regularly. But what if you're starting from scratch—on a first-time hunt for the perfect job? What if you're going back to work after a hiatus? What if you've decided retirement isn't for you? In all three cases, it's realistic to assume your strategy may require a different plan. That's not to say the lessons put forth thus far are not valuable to each group; they are designed to move every business professional forward. But you may have to take a different tack, especially as you enter the networking arena.

TAKE STOCK

Whether you're a first-timer, second-timer or old-timer, you have something of value to offer the business community. So, as you wonder "Where do I start?", take stock of your professional assets and hone in on a specific goal. It doesn't matter if you're just out of college or have been out of work for an extended period of time. What counts is that you're you and no one else can offer the workplace exactly what you can provide.

Grab pencil and paper and itemize what you've got going for you. Include your personal attributes, business experiences and what you feel you can bring to the party—your untapped potential. I don't care if you're ninety, you still have untapped potential! The exercises in earlier chapters helped you to identify your professional potential and explore suitable job opportunities. What's different about this assignment is you'll want to pay special attention to those experiences that bear your unique touch.

One of the young college graduates I helped counsel told me he had an unusual way of leading others. He was often head camp counselor, head lifeguard or head-something. He made whatever team he was put in charge of meet weekly to collaborate on any new guidelines that would help them do a better job. He told them it was up to them to make policy additions and changes, even though he was the designated leader. His work as a young facilitator was clearly one of his strengths. As he made his list, he realized his approach to leading was unorthodox. This was only one item on his inventory sheet, but a very impressive and powerful one. I told him to keep going. Although he was young by industry standards, he had quite a few meaningful experiences to bring to any company.

For those who have already been in the workplace—second-timers or old-timers—your list should be comprised of past on-the-job accomplishments and wins that were creative, innovative and results-oriented. These are very important to any prospective employer, and they also remind you how lucky that new employer will be to find you. No matter who you are as a business professional, standing back and taking an objective look at where you've come from and what you've done provides a wonderful boost, something we all need.

HOLD YOUR HEAD UP

I was told by the crème de la crème of headhunters that a strong sense of self-confidence was the underlying selling feature of every one of their candidates. Confidence is doubly important when you're playing the job-hunting game with a "handicap." Let's face it, trying to nail that first job or trying to land one after a sabbatical, isn't as easy as it is for those with considerable experience or who have remained active in the workplace. If the hiring party is a bit hesitant, sway them in your direction with your strong sense of self. They are comparing you to other candidates, the majority of whom are currently employed or recently unemployed. As you're taking stock of all you have to offer, make a separate list of why you should feel confident about

yourself. Make it a subheading under "personal attributes."

I have to share a funny story: A girlfriend of mine had left the business world to raise her three children. She vowed to wait until the youngest reached kindergarten before she resumed her career. She hadn't worked for eight years. She was once a top salesperson, selling paper supplies for Boise Cascade. The time off played havoc with her level of personal confidence, but here's how she handled it: She called every close friend and those she'd stayed in touch with over the years from her last job, and asked them what they liked about her as a business professional. She took notes. "Now, be honest with me," she chided. She kept her list taped inside the cover of her day planner and read it every morning. She claims that exercise reinstated her good feelings about herself. (By the way, she got job offers from all five companies to which she applied. All this took place within four weeks of her reemergence into the job market.)

I have another friend, a real nut (in the fun way), who threw a dinner party for himself and invited a dozen of his closest friends. They were as playful as he was, so agreed to center the table conversation around the positives about my friend. "The only dialogue you can engage in has to be about me. And it has to be positive," he instructed. He permitted them to tell him and the others how terrific he was. This was done through occasional toasts, favorite stories (that extolled his virtues) and flat-out compliments. After dinner, they were allowed to talk about other things. The dinner setting created an intimate atmosphere, and everyone's attention stayed focused on Phil. (He made sure everyone visited the restrooms before they sat down, because no one could leave the table). Not only was this event uplifting for Phil, but they all had a lot of laughs. Phil later told me that several of his friends copied him. Phil videotaped this confidence-boosting event and tells me he still plays it. Wouldn't you?

If your self-confidence is a little rusty, assess what can you do to make sure it's firmly in place before you take the workplace by storm!

A FIRST TIME FOR EVERYTHING

If you're fresh out of school and looking for your first real career opportunity, how do you network your way into the circle of contacts you need? In addition to following each of the assignments laid out in earlier chapters, immediately contact a headhunter, employment agency or career counselor. If you're not sure how to find one or all of these groups, start with the library, the phone book's yellow pages, or a local chamber of commerce. Colleges also have career counseling centers and network contacts you can utilize.

As you get into the swing of going on interviews, start establishing some relationships other than the ones I talked about in previous chapters. Tell yourself you will make one casual acquaintance at every interview you go on. This could include staying in touch with the receptionist you chatted with while waiting for an interview or the secretary to the human resource director. You also can go to lunch from time to time with the contact you found at the employment agency. Getting them in a quiet, relaxed setting may stimulate helpful conversation—dialogue that could help you gain more contacts and insight. Another good idea is to hang out with friends who are business professionals, whether or not they work in your field of interest, and begin meeting people in their worlds.

We all have to start somewhere, so take your networking chores one day at a time. If, at the end of each week, you can account for broadening your networking base, you're well on your way. Just make sure you check up on yourself to test your progress. Do you seem to be spinning in a circle? Do you feel like you've made little progress from the prior week in networking toward that job? Then count up the number of contacts you've accumulated. I bet if you're adding people to your treasured list, you're getting somewhere professionally—i.e., more interviews. Make it your goal to double your contacts each week. If one week you make one, the next week vow to collect two. I think you become downhearted only when you're not expanding. Measure your success by the amount of people you're getting to know.

A lot of young people are uncomfortable reaching out for help along the way, but don't be. Think of it this way: We all like to help one another. Would you mind helping someone who was on their way to the job they wanted? Don't be afraid to ask for what you need to get that networking database going. It is through this collection of contacts that you will find career opportunities throughout your life.

If you decide to skip some of the homework assignments from earlier chapters, don't forego seeking out a mentor. Having someone in your corner who you can go for coaching and a little cheerleading is one of the best things you can do for yourself. That may be true for all of us, but it's especially true if you're a first-timer.

If you're between eighteen and twenty-four, try to visualize yourself at least ten years older when you sit across the desk at an interview or while on the phone with a networking contact. Lack of sophistication can be a minus. It's not unusual to lack a certain amount of poise and presence at young ages, but it's necessary to give the impression that we are mature professionals. If you visualize being a little older, your body language tends to reflect that. In the end, it's all part of that confidence thing. I am always impressed with young people when I suddenly realize I'm not at all aware of their age, just aware of them and who they are.

THE SECOND TIME AROUND

For many, reentering the workplace is no big deal, but for others, it's frightening and mysteriously depressing. Many have taken time to raise families, while others decided to travel, and there are some who fell ill and were forced to take time off.

If you fall into the second-timer category, you need to get your momentum going. It's hard to make such a drastic change in your life—to be doing one thing, then suddenly another. To make such a change takes a great deal of effort, especially when it comes to shifting your mindset—to have it go from what you've *been* doing to what you *will be* doing. If you're a second-timer, your first task is to "think" career again to get your momentum going.

Many second-timers can start the networking process by contacting old business colleagues and friends to see what opportunities might fit their capabilities. But what if you've lost contact? What if you haven't stayed in touch over the years? You can check with a couple of good headhunters, read the classifieds under your job description, check the Web and talk to friends who work for companies that interest you. One of the best things you can do immediately is to rejoin industry-related clubs, associations and groups to which you once belonged. Chances are good that you will be reunited with some of those old contacts through such affiliations. You also can run an ad about yourself on a Web page or industry business journal so those interested in what

you have to offer can get in touch with you.

What's most important for a second-timer to remember is that you've already made your mark. You know how to move about in the business world, and, as you reenter the business community, you have the distinct pleasure of anticipating moving ahead toward career goals that you had to put on hold for whatever reason. This would also be a terrific time to reassess your professional goals to see whether you want to change direction. If not, take a close look at how far you want to go in the profession you're in and how you want to rekindle your former career. In view of your past, your future is bright; that alone is a great feeling. All you need to do now is get active and begin networking again.

People reentering the workplace often feel awkward at first, but it's that getting-back-on-the-bicycle thing; in a short time, you'll feel right at home making the rounds in the business community.

Your first venture should be carefully chosen. It should be an event that makes you feel welcome and enthused. I know a business associate who traveled in Asia for a year and picked up where he left off when he returned. He called his old service club, the Elks, (who threw him a good-bye lunch before leaving town) and went to their weekly meetings for a month. He did this before even beginning to look for a job. Reinstating past relationships made him feel like no time had lapsed at all. The sense of fellowship helped launch him back into the workplace with a wonderful backboard of support. He also got a real feel for what was going on business-wise within his community. He contacted each member between meetings to network with them; and all of them provided productive leads. My friend was in the landscape maintenance business—maintaining the grounds for large companies, industrial properties and residential communities—and it wasn't long before he renewed old ties and developed new ties. Within six months he was well on his way to rebuilding the business he had shut down a year before. By year's end, he had more clients than he had the first time around, and he had built *that* original customer base for six years. He told me the Elk Club was largely responsible for helping him get back on his feet.

If you're a second-timer, what relationships and associations can you rekindle? Sure, you can hedge your bets by contacting a headhunter or seeking out networking contacts through friend and family, but what did you leave behind? Go back and reconnect. You paid your dues; now's it's time to cash in.

WHAT? ME RETIRE?

"So long as someone has a superb attitude, I would much rather hire an older person, any day," said a printing company executive friend. "The combination of their work and life experiences are invaluable to me—to any employer." Many other company owners told me essentially the same thing.

If you're an old-timer, what you have to offer the workplace has little competition. The younger set can't compete with your work-related experiences, and they don't have your maturity. Plus, you've probably accumulated more contacts throughout your life.

If you're healthy, have taken good care of yourself and have a positive attitude, you're probably needed and wanted in more jobs than you can imagine. Also, a lot of people want your name on their networking list, which makes it easy for you to get their name on yours. But the great news is that you have accumulated a bank

full of friends, acquaintances and business associates after your years in the business community. You've proven yourself, and you're worth your background in gold. Your contacts are there for the taking and the using, so whatever you want to do will be easier to achieve because you have more fish in your pond. I have more reverence for those older than me because I know they're usually smarter, wiser and more tolerant. To them, I always listen.

Many think they are useless in the business world after a certain age because they have fallen prey to media hype that emphasizes youth. But many human resource directors would rather have wisdom over fewer birthday candles any day.

Here's another plus for the old-timer. We're just starting in an age where the "consultant" is the rage. Many old-timers are retired and in a perfect place to work as consultants. If you have expertise in any field, and can advise, counsel or train in it, you're going to be sought out time and again if you let people know you're available. Consultants can usually pick and choose the jobs they want, and they can often choose how frequently they wish to work at them.

Most old-timers have experience in more than one area of professional interest and can select one or all to do in their later years. I know a judge who's retired and works on a "rent-a-judge" basis. He only wants to oversee cases that deal with medical malpractice, his favorite; now he enjoys doing what he loves every time he works. He has become a highly reputed judicial figure to those who seek his services, so he's cashing in on experience and reputation.

Professionally, this is the best time of your life. It often takes years for business professionals to earn respect in their industries. There is no better time in your career to enjoy your contacts and professional inventory than when you become an old-timer. The good judge confided to me that, at sixty-seven, he finally felt fulfilled and happy with his work. He also had amassed a Rolodex of contacts that could fill a bank vault.

If you haven't kept good records, go back over your life and see if you can reconstruct some of your lists of names. Pick a client, job, business associate or company with which you were once affiliated and go back and work those contacts. Of course, this time keep fastidious records!

Review your vast experience that has given you to offer what no other person in your field has. This is what will impress a potential employer. We sometimes forget the worth of our life and work experiences. Take stock, count those blessings and appreciate all you've done with your professional life. Ask yourself who will benefit most from what you have to offer, then find them. Go back to work and enjoy what may well be the best years of your life. And keep in mind what Satchel Page once said: "If you didn't know how old you were, how old would you be?"

LET'S RECAP
For All Three Groups

1. Count your blessings. Take stock of personal attributes and business experiences.

2. Decide on a specific goal, and be clear about it.

3. After making your list of attributes and work-related experiences, detail what you can offer the business world that is unique and special.

4. List those things that represent major on-the-job accomplishments from your work history.

5. Boost that self-confidence by listing your strengths. Ask yourself and those who know

you why you should feel confident. Keep these notes in a subhead file under "personal attributes." Make sure they're within view, and review them frequently.

6. Do the homework assignments in earlier chapters. All of them are geared for people just like you.

7. Remember: No one can provide exactly what you can provide the workplace; there's only one of you.

For the First-Timer

1. Contact a headhunter, employment agency or career counselor.

2. Make acquaintances with any individuals who can help you, including the above group or the receptionist where you just interviewed. Invite them to go to lunch with you for additional contacts and insight and to build that networking base.

3. Hang out with friends who are business professionals, even if their profession isn't your cup of tea. It's a great way to meet people and kick off your networking campaign.

4. Count your number of new contacts weekly. They should double each time.

5. Find yourself a mentor. This can be any business professional for whom you have great respect. Let them help guide you as you work your way toward that job you want.

6. Envision yourself ten years older. It gives you a sense of maturity and professionalism.

7. Remember: You're young and you've got a wonderful professional life ahead of you. Start building your future.

For the Second-Timer

1. Contact old business associates, colleagues and friends and ask what's happening.

2. Get in touch with a headhunter. Run an ad

about yourself on the Web or in a business trade publication.

3. Rejoin clubs, associations and groups that were beneficial to your career and industry interests last time around.

4. Assess your professional goals. Do you want to change direction? If not, how far do you want to go in your current career?

5. Get active and begin networking wherever you smell opportunity.

6. Make sure your first venture back into the business community makes you feel welcome and enthused.

7. What personal and professional associations can you rekindle? Go back and reconnect.

8. Remember: You've already made your mark in the business world. It should be easier the second time around.

For the Old-Timer

1. You have little competition when it comes to work-related experiences. The older you are and the more you've worked, the more valuable you are to the business world.

2. You've got more wisdom and contacts than most people looking for jobs. Enjoy and work them both.

3. Employers everywhere are looking for people just like you: There's no substitute for experience or for a fat rolodex of networking contacts.

4. You live in an age when the consultant is the rage. What can you advise, counsel or train in? Capitalize on it!

5. Reconstruct a list of key people from your past who can help you realize your professional dreams.

6. Make a detailed list of what you can give an employer that no one else with your supposed skills can offer. Go ahead, boast a little; you've earned it.

7. Chances are you've amassed enough experience to choose from more than one job description in your field. Be picky, and choose the one you want.

8. Remember: Because of your age you've accumulated hundreds of contacts. You're the envy on the networking block. Enjoy that privileged position, and use it to your advantage.

There's really not a lot of difference between these three groups and those who are already in the business world—just a few hurdles to overcome. Focus on the positives and lock out all negative thoughts.

Every working business professional has some type of "handicap" they need to overcome and work around. With determination, creativity and perseverance, any obstacle can be overcome. Lean toward the positives as you venture into the job market. You have just as good a chance—maybe even better—than most people out there.

chapter twelve

Big City vs. Little Town

Some say you need to be in a big city to make a successful career happen, while others disagree, especially in this highly technological age where communication knows no boundaries. The truth is, there are ups and downs to working and networking in the small town and the large city. No matter where you find yourself, neither environment has to be limiting or overwhelming.

MAKING THE ROUNDS
IN LITTLE TOWNS

If you prefer the slower pace of a small town, there are pros and cons to networking. On the plus side, the smaller the pond, the more fish you know. On the con side, with few fish there's fewer opportunities.

Although the group may be small, working with those contacts can be a real advantage. One positive aspect is you can get to know everyone on a more intimate basis. Smaller communities are normally more close-knit. Many small-town professionals feel a sense of family, because ev-

eryone is willing to help one another and share their networking leads.

When you're networking in a smaller community, your job is to become an "insider"—to get to know everybody who is anybody. That includes schmoozing with the mayor, the city council and every business leader in town. Most small towns have the same things big towns have—banks, retail centers, manufacturing and medical facilities—and some even specialize in a particular industry. Get to know all the business leaders by joining clubs and organizations that promote business. Those affiliations provide excellent networking breaks.

Tap into whatever power sources run your town, as well. One person I talked to in Wyoming said that Myrtle, the general-store clerk, was the networking source extraordinaire. She knew all the goings-on in town and was very well connected. Get to know the movers and shakers like Myrtle in your small community.

But as you do, one word of caution: In a small town it is easy to alienate those you need in your networking circle. If you gossip about the heads of the PTA at a business lunch and her husband happens to know the person sitting next to you, that information might get transferred quickly. As that news travels, it just might cross the ears of the wrong person—maybe your boss, for instance, who is a friend of hers. Also, if you make a fool of yourself at the company picnic in a small town, that's another SOS that could be picked up by the person you may one day want to work for. On the downside, then, a small town requires that your sense of PR stay intact at all times.

Very often, moving up the business ladder is contingent upon who you know. After talking to a number of people on this subject, I've found that politics are the same in any size city. Image and profile are key no matter where you live.

On the plus side, it's much easier to rub shoulders with the power brokers in a smaller town because they're usually just a few network contacts away.

It's also easy to make contacts in other ways in a small town. Coaching your child's Little League team, for instance. Such casual acquaintances can easily lead to networking sources and good friends that last a lifetime. Social and civic involvement provide wonderful opportunities for making viable contacts.

And what about charity work? Every single community across America has organizations that help those in need. Besides making you feel good about yourself, there are people—important people—who take part in such good works. Your job is to get to know them.

Take advantage of all that's available to you in your small town. The key to doing that, I'm told, is to stay active within the community professionally, socially and politically.

If you're a small-towner, your task is to get to know one person in every facet within the community. Soon you will establish a prestigious networking base.

PLANT SEEDS

Over the years I've had a long-distance working relationship with a woman named Christine who worked for a small specialty promotion company in Santa Rosa, California. The company made merchandising elements like baseball caps and sweatshirts for sports entities, such as high school and college athletic teams. Christine worked with major companies in big cities nationwide because of the nature of her work, so she had many chances to make great networking contacts. Still, she had to rely on the community in which she was based to produce the company's product line. She readily received whatever she needed from other local businesspersons because she knew everyone in town. Christine confided to me that she received no less than two job offers each month from those she dealt with in Santa Rosa because everyone she came in contact with saw her as a real go-getter. She earned quite a reputation and had built a networking base of all the locals.

When Christine finally decided that she had outgrown her current job and wanted something more challenging, she already had a strong networking circle to turn to—people who knew her personality and work ethic. After she made a conscious decision to move on, she began to "work" her contacts. This was easy because Christine knew everyone in the business community and was active in everything in town. As she attended various functions and activities, she began to investigate what might be available in the way of interesting job opportunities. She scouted jobs and resources that might help her land the one she wanted.

Through a series of queries, pitching her

package, and just happening to be in the right place at the right time, Christine eventually landed a great job for a private wine grower (Santa Rosa is in California's wine country) as assistant to the president. Though she hadn't set out for that particular job, she came upon it through her networking search.

Christine later told me the position turned out to be the dream job of a lifetime, one she would be content with throughout her career. She had the best of everything—the family atmosphere a small town could provide, a great place to raise her children, a job she loved and a salary equal to what she would have made working in a big city.

Anyone can do what Christine did. If you're ambitious enough and work your contacts, you can create innumerable opportunities for yourself. Christine kept asking, "Who do I know that. . . ." She worked with all she had and reaped great returns for the efforts she expended. Even in a small town, a broad base of contacts increases the odds that you'll move up. Like Christine, that career move may come when you least expect it, from a source you hadn't even imagined.

One of the things Christine did so well was utilizing all the contacts she made within her community. She got to know many people in larger towns and cities, too, who counseled her about their experiences in the business world. She gathered momentum, made contacts and persevered until she got to the finish line. It took about a year before she found her dream job, and she worked at it every day, taking advantage of her networking base.

Another advantage to working your way up in a small town is that you can get to the top faster and move to a bigger pond with greater ease. Should you ever wish to take those credentials to the big city, you've positioned yourself well for entry at a higher level when you make that move. If you're assistant to the company president, it looks great on your resume whether that town has twenty thousand, two hundred thousand or two million people.

If you already live in a small town or are planning to relocate to one, do what Christine did. Work your contacts, get to know as many people as you can through your job (whether they live in your town or not) and keep your ear to the ground. In Christine's case, she asked around to see what jobs were up for grabs. It was her diligence and sense of purpose that created an opportunity she never expected. Like Christine, you may stumble upon more than one fantasy job that you never even dreamed of, if you keep plugging away.

CITY SLICKER

The big city is quite different from a small town. Some say more insensitive, some say more interesting. It can be either or both, depending on your perceptions. Whatever your point of view, your success in a big city depends largely on learning to manipulate that city's resources. It also relies just as heavily on your intent, perseverance and how consistently you penetrate the many layers a big city has. Frankly, I don't see much difference in the dynamic of a large city vs. a small town. People are people. But in a big city, networking your way around requires more persistence and drive, more stamina and a thicker skin. It also takes more time.

There is something about a big city that can make you feel incidental. Big cities just seem, well, so big in comparison to little ones. Knowing how to take advantage of sources is not always easy unless you've grown up there. But you can learn the pulse and groove of the big city by observing the way others do it. A great place to start is to attend industry functions—meetings and social events that cater to your career interests. This is the most positive way to begin your networking base.

There are many advantages to the big city: a plethora of jobs from which to choose, lots of openings and more people to meet, which translates into more networking contacts. One of the greatest benefits of working in the big city is that you're at the heartbeat of innovation; you often find yourself in trendsetting circles. Most executives are impressed when an applicant has worked in a city like Los Angeles or New York and held a position for a large company such as IBM or Bank One. If the applicant could be successful despite a great deal of competition for good jobs, he obviously was on the ball to land that job in the first place.

But networking and building a career in the big city has its set of limitations. Getting that job you want may take a little longer because there is more of everything: more careers to pursue; more jobs to check out; more companies to look into; more competition (allowing employers to be choosy) and more job offers. Building networking contacts to make all this happen can also take longer, since people are not as apt to get back to you as quickly. Unfortunately, it may take longer to get a meeting with an important contact. Big cities tend to breed a frantic pace and where there's freneticism there's always a shortage of time. Be patient as you network your way to the job you want in the big city.

LOCATION, LOCATION, LOCATION

I discussed earlier how important it was to choose a work location that would be conducive to your peace of mind. I was talking about your job being reasonably close to home, especially if

you can't hack the stress of a daily long-distance drive. Now let's discuss how to find a work environment first and a home to go with it later. You need to decide whether a big city or small town suits your fancy because where you plant yourself geographically will affect the mechanics of how you network.

For some of us, where we work will be decided for us. Perhaps your company decides to transfer you. If you like your job, you'll most likely make the move. But this category of business professionals represents only a small segment of the business world. For the rest of us, including those just entering the job market or wanting to make a career move, selecting a location may be a tough decision. But I caution you: It's a key factor that needs to be considered up front because your networking strategy depends on it.

Be aware that choosing a new or different geographical place to work can impact your entire future. Such a decision, particularly early on in a career, has long-range effects. Most people don't want to budge, so they'll work within a familiar region. Only a small percentage make a move from one state to another, and if they do, it's usually because of a job transfer.

There are those, however, who want to venture out and explore beyond where they've been before, whether it's a rustic little town or a large, fast-paced city. In either case, there are distinctive differences in how the networking game is played and how the whole process works. Getting a good grasp of those idiosyncrasies is essential, if not critical.

TO MOVE OR NOT TO MOVE

As you explore suitable job opportunities and pinpoint your professional direction, you'll learn that your choices can only make sense if they correlate with your career objectives. Ask yourself if what you want to do is where you're at, literally. In other words, are you in the right place territorially for the right things to happen to you professionally? Are there plentiful networking opportunities available to you? If not, don't panic; it doesn't matter nearly as much as knowing how to utilize the resources you do have available. But having more opporunities will make your search easier.

I know a guy from the Midwest who is a hospital administrator. His small town of a few thousand has one hospital. He realized that if he wanted to move up (he hoped to eventually be at the helm of such a facility) he would have to leave his current position and relocate to a large city with a number of similar medical facilities. Scared as he was to move to "the city," he realized where he lived and worked offered few networking opportunities to get him the job he ultimately wanted. After careful deliberation, he knew he would have to make a physical move to reach his career goal.

Take a good look at the odds of advancing your career in the town you're currently working or about to work. You need to determine if there are enough networking sources, as well—the kind to help you find the job you want or to move you forward along your career path. This is not to say that you can't make substantial contacts if you choose to work in a small town. To the contrary, I interviewed a number of business professionals who live in small towns and network outside their geographical scope to do big things.

One of my friends lives in a Pacific coast village and designs aviation systems. Most of his work is done on computer. The Los Angeles-based company he works for requires only that he attend monthly meetings, so he is able to enjoy the environs of his choice as well as his work, all the while pulling down a six-figure salary. His job requires seeking out technology on the cutting edge, so he is forced to network daily. He does so mostly through the Internet.

Another associate of mine is an architect. He lives in Santa Fe, New Mexico, but designs commercial buildings for companies in Chicago, Atlanta and Minneapolis. He, too, relies on computer technology and travels when his clients demand it. He admits he travels more than he would like (a couple times a week), but that's the trade-off. He also networks by phone and religiously dedicates half a day out of his weekly schedule to networking with sources who can lead to additional business.

Your first assignment is to determine where you think you'll be most happy and productive: a small town or a big city. After deciding on size, pick where that might be in the country. Some prefer the East Coast or West Coast, while others want the Midwest only. Some want the biggest of cities, while others want city life in a more pared down version. If you think a small town is the optimal atmosphere, pinpoint which one, in what region of the country. After making that crucial decision, you can set up networking goals and chip away at them. Consider whether you're willing to sacrifice lifestyle for career. Does your career take precedence over where you live, or can you make some compromises to have both? If so, identify what those "gives for gets" might be.

For many, moving for career's sake is all right in the formative years of career building, but later on, most opt for lifestyle over career. Maybe getting the job you want means choosing a career that will support your choice of locale.

Many who work in a big city and live in the surrounding small suburbs say they have the ideal life. Others claim the trek from the burbs to the big town is tiring and takes too much of their leisure time.

WHEN BIG THINGS TAKE US FROM LITTLE PLACES

Sometimes to fulfill our career wishes, we have to move to a large city; there's no way around it. Some opportunities for various careers are just not available in a small town. For instance, if you want to be in show business you have to go to an "industry" town such as Los Angeles or New York if you really hope to make it. No matter how much performing experience you get elsewhere, you have to be where the action is to become celebrated. If you're an attorney and want to be with a large environmental law firm, you won't find one in Fargo, North Dakota. If you hope to work in network news, staying at an affiliate television station in Bend, Oregon, won't make that happen. Sometimes our career goals require leaving a small town for a big city. The adjustment can be grueling.

How do you get ahead if you're in that boat? Essentially, you do the same things you would in a small town. Perhaps you won't get in to see the mayor, but you can try to make friends with someone in the mayor's office if such an affiliation would boost your career. If not, look at sources that will move you forward. Do the exercises in chapter five before you even land in the big city. Like a good scout, you want to be prepared.

Your first stop when you hit the city streets should be to check in with some reputable headhunters and employment firms that place people in your field. Next, read all the local media—trade journals, magazines and newspapers—and see if you can pinpoint what major companies are experiencing sales in-

creases and growth. Kick off your networking effort by sending them your package.

As I mentioned earlier, become affiliated with industry groups and associations; they're at the core of your networking base. Align yourself with a charity or civic organization. Several top-level executives told me such affiliations proved to be the most lucrative of all in terms of building their networking contacts. Many such charitable groups are directly tied to your industry. In fact, I know of no industry networking organization that isn't affiliated with a charity of some kind. These organizations could open doors for you that you hadn't thought possible.

One good thing about choosing the big city over the little town is that you have more resources at your fingertips than you can probably ever use or need. But ultimately, the choice of where to practice your profession is strictly up to you. Revisit chapter two; many of your answers to these worksheet questions will clarify what size venue you need to satisfy your career goals and objectives.

TIPS FOR NETWORKING IN A SMALL TOWN

1. Become an insider by getting to know anybody who is somebody: the mayor, city council members and other prestigious figures in the community.

2. Make friends with all the major business leaders in your town.

3. Join clubs, groups and organizations that promote business growth and opportunity.

4. Determine whether or not you have an interesting person like Myrtle, the general store clerk, in your community. If so, get to know that person. Contact them frequently to get the latest scoop.

5. Coach a Little League team or be a scout

leader—something you can do with your family that will provide opportunities to meet people you would not otherwise come in contact with.

6. Volunteer your help or services for a local charity group.

7. Stay active in your community professionally, socially and politically.

8. Reach outside your community to larger cities and towns, and see how you can utilize those sources to further your career goals or increase your knowledge about the business world.

9. Get to know someone in every facet within your community, including business, social, religious and political circles. Have at least one contact in every pocket of your small town.

TIPS FOR NETWORKING IN THE BIG CITY

1. Learn to manipulate and maneuver the resources available in your city of choice.

2. Remember that you need thick skin and adequate amounts of drive, stamina, persistence and patience to stay in the big city's competitive game, so gear up. Keep yourself inspired with positive thoughts, people and ideas.

3. Observe the culture of the city by attending industry functions and events. Go to meetings and social events, which will launch your bank of networking contacts.

4. A city offers more jobs to choose from, more job openings, more people to meet and the chance to enjoy trendsetting innovations. Seize each opportunity.

5. Make friends as high up as the mayor's office. Schmooze with as many heavy hitters as you can.

6. Engage the services of a headhunter or employment agency prior to settling down in the city. They can help you hit the ground running.

7. Read local media such as trade journals, magazines and newspapers. Contact the companies with growth and sales increases.

8. Affiliate with at least one industry group.

9. Offer your time and talents to a local charity. Make as many contacts through this organization as you can. Remember to choose a group in need that is somehow related to your work interests.

No matter which way you're leaning—small town or big city—there are many different ways to network your way to the job you want. The key is to stay motivated and positive, resourceful and industrious. Wherever you're located, there will be people and where there are people, there are always opportunities to network.

Use your creativity. Go beyond the obvious to network in your small town or big city. Use your imagination and do the networking thing a little differently or with a new twist. Go beyond the prescribed tips. Make a list of your own, and see what other ideas you can come up with to network that weren't mentioned in the punchlist tip sheet. File those ideas away in your wonderfully organized filing system or database. At some point in your career, you may want to go back and review those notes.

chapter thirteen

Weighing the Job Choices

Now that you've done a stellar job interviewing, you have no doubt received several job offers. It's time then to decide which one will fit your personal and professional needs. For some, a job choice may be a snap, but more often than not, making a choice between even two job offers can be agonizing. Each job may have equally attractive features. You can choose only one, and the choice you make will be a life-altering decision, so you want to be sure you make the right one. This is where, once again, your networking skills come into play. You don't have to make such weighty decisions by yourself; bounce the pros and cons off colleagues, mentors, friends, family and others to reach a comfortable decision. Seek out everyone on your people list who is in the field or knows someone in it. From there, make a few calls, schedule a few meetings and see what input you can gather. You will gain a tremendous amount of insight into what choices are suitable for your goals and needs. It's a great way to check out the upsides and downsides of each offer.

AND THE LIST GOES ON

Reach for pencil and paper again. Record your thoughts and ideas, and note the networking contacts who can help with your job consideration process as I've just mentioned. There are lots of factors to consider, too.

Sit down with all your job offers, and itemize the pros and cons of each job. Any offer that has a neon negative attached to it should be promptly dismissed. But when you're just not sure, there are several ways to get to the finish line.

For starters, make a list of what is negative and what is positive—from a subjective point of view—about each of your job offers. Match those answers to what you know you really want and what you simply could not deal with. Eliminate jobs that aren't even close to possibilities, whether it's because of location, salary, amount of hours you'll need to work, unappealing or nonstimulating tasks, the company's culture, lack of job advancement, or job responsibilities that won't further your knowledge and growth. I had a friend who wanted a job in real estate, working in the sales office for new homes. She found the perfect job—days and hours she wanted, salary, a product she could get behind—but it was quite a distance away. She had to come to grips with driving over two hours every day. When she was realistic and objective about it, she knew it would become stressful over time. Since she had to work for this home builder for a minimum of eighteen months, possibly longer (until the homes were completely sold), she realized she wouldn't be able to hack it. It was a sad realization, yes, but the sacrifice was just too much. She had small children and wanted to be closer to home. Also, she disliked the arduous freeway trek. She had to pass and did so right away. That one negative was something she couldn't overlook. Don't pass up something more suitable while you take a road-to-nowhere detour; that can only result in a dead end. And if you take that side trip for a short time, chances are your second choice—the more practical one—may be gone by the time you call back to accept it.

One of the difficulties in weighing job choices is that they often come all at once. You're in the job market to get a job, and if you're actively interviewing, which you should be, you may feel bombarded with offers. If you can take a time-out and step back to assess all the particulars, you'll be more apt to make a sound decision rather than an impulsive one. Most experts seem to follow these rules:

Rule Number One: Don't take the first thing that comes along unless you're truly in love with it.

Rule Number Two: Make sure you thoroughly rank the pros and cons of each offer. Sometimes what makes us leave a job soon after we've accepted it isn't even on our list. I've seen many people scribble their lists in haste, and as a result, forget some of the good and bad points. Then they are disappointed when they have to deal with the bad ones, sooner than later.

Rule Number Three: Be objective. It's hard not to be subjective because job offers bring out the emotional side in many of us. It's like being in love; we can't see beyond that immediate, overwhelming, swept-off-our-feet sensation. We focus on what is great about a job, without standing back and examining every detail. That's not to say that you shouldn't go with your gut feeling about a job. My colleague, Carol Cranfield, places hundreds of business professionals a year and tells her clients (on both sides) that 75 percent of their decision should be based on chemistry. "If the circumstances don't feel right, then don't bother," she says. "The people you work with are like extended family." Without exception, harmony and synergy are two things that must be foremost in the mix. But even with the chemistry there, make a careful assessment of the pluses and minuses before you take the job. Your acceptance is a major commitment.

So make that list, and check it more than once. Write down your thoughts, leave it for a day or two, then go back over it. You may have a bolt of enlightenment; you may come upon other aspects, positive or negative. A job is something you will spend more time on than with your significant other, your children possibly and that precious time you get with yourself; make sure you'll like doing the job you choose. At a minimum, you'll be doing it no less than 2,064 hours a year. Most of us have less than half that amount of time during the week for other activities, excluding sleep. Who wants to look back one day and regret having taken a job that kept you from your real potential, or caused you to waste even a few of your precious hours?

YOU'VE GOT A FRIEND

It's true that no one lives your life but you, but we all have at least one trusted friend to whom we can turn when trying to make any decision, large or small. We don't have to choose a job alone. Sure, you can talk to your husband or wife, your children or your roommate, but nothing is more valuable than calling upon that person who knows you like no other. Ferret out the friend who knows you well and for a long time. Talk to the one who will give you unbiased feedback. This is the person who knows your strengths and weaknesses, who knows you at your best and worst, who knows your temperament well and who has supported you in your life's dreams. Usually, it's the friend who has known you most of your life. My closest friend, Judy, is someone I see only a few times a year, yet she has been my most trusted friend since we were in seventh grade. When I am making a life-changing decision, she's where I go. I know she won't give me a bunch of baloney and tell me what she thinks I want to hear. Though she's always sensitive and diplomatic, she is direct and honest in her observations, which is what I want. It helps me see things clearly.

What you may want to do is call your most trusted friend and let them know to be on standby (especially if it's someone you don't talk to regularly). Tell him or her you're looking for a job and need someone you can access quickly for a heart-to-heart and who can help you assess each opportunity. That should get the friend thinking about you and what would be best for you in terms of the right job. So by the time you do call for that serious chat, your friend is primed and ready. I actually prefer calling Judy because we don't talk every day. For that reason, I feel she has a more detached view of my life. I cannot think of one instance when her perception wasn't accurate when it came to assisting me with critical decisions. You, too, may want to consult with someone from childhood with whom you've kept a close relationship—someone you've been closely involved with but don't speak to or see all the time.

You may be one of those people who doesn't like to ask for things because you feel you're imposing on people and you're a burden, but put yourself in their place. You know if it was that special friend needing your help in sorting through a handful of job offers, you'd be right there. Whatever side you're on—asking or receiving advice on decisions that important—it tends to bring out an individual's deepest wisdom and analytical side. These are excellent attributes to get or to give when helping or being helped by a friend. So don't be afraid to take your pros and cons to a friend, lay them out before him or her and spend time looking at each offer from every angle; that's what friends are for.

GURUS, MENTORS AND OTHER WISE PEOPLE

One more way to assure you're making a judicious choice with that job selection is to talk with a person you consider to be your mentor. This individual should be someone senior to you in either age or experience and who knows the business community where you're headed. As I mentioned at the beginning of the chapter, your networking skills will come in handy once again. Ask yourself who you know that has had this job, knows the industry well and can illuminate what you can or should expect in choosing a particular job.

I have a good friend who had a lifelong

dream of being a firefighter. He worked hard in several other jobs for eight years until he was ready and able to apply in this field. Before he took that final step, though, he contacted a friend of a friend of a friend who'd been fighting fires for twelve years and asked him to lunch. Now that my friend had his chance to take this job—he had been accepted and the offer was on the table—he still wanted to make certain he was making the right choice. The guy he was meeting with knew several of the firefighters at the station house where my friend was to work, and knew that location's operation well. My friend spent two hours virtually interviewing the expert. That conversation was the deciding factor that swayed my friend to take that job over one other.

You can do what he did and talk with someone who works in the field or knows the dynamics within the company from which you've received an offer. Make your list of questions ahead of time so you won't forget something.

You can also talk to those wise people in your life, including your minister, your career counselor, the headhunter who helped you get the offer in the first place or even your therapist or astrologer. Whoever has guided you at different pivotal times down your path—who is not necessarily a friend—is another excellent avenue for processing your options.

Get as much advice as you think you need, then sift it through your own filter to see what resonates with you. This will provide an expanded view as you weigh and measure your job options.

Experts say at least half the people in the business community substantially slow down their career growth and advancement for no other reason than for having taken the wrong job for an indefinite period of time. "Haste makes waste," as Ben Franklin often said.

ASSESS THE COMPANY'S FUTURE

Carol Cranfield emphasizes shifting your weight toward the job that offers financial stability. She stresses that no one should ever choose a job because of salary—that should be the last reason—but inquire as to whether or not the company is solid. Cranfield says don't worry about your own salary as much as the worth and stability of the company you're going to work for. You can always get promotions and raises if a company has substantial worth and credible backing. If they're a fly-by-night operation, it does little to list them on your resume and a great deal to waste your career momentum.

Cranfield also feels that when you take a job, it should be with the intention of staying for some time. Therefore, your choice should also be based on what the position will do to enhance your career goals as you look ahead to the bigger picture.

Contact the local chamber of commerce to see if the company is a member. Most solid companies are, and the chamber can give you background information on them. You can also snoop around to see if you know anyone who works at your company of interest. See what they say about the stability, growth, management strategies—whatever is important to you and your goals. Also, see what trade organizations or associations have to say about the company. Placement and employment agencies may be able to tell you what they know about the company. If an agency sent you on the interview in the first place, they will know a great deal about them. Finally, when at the company, notice what awards and commendations they have received for their work and participation in the community. As you

I WILL WEIGH MY JOB OFFERS ACCORDING TO THE FOLLOWING:

1. The job offer of _____ at _____
   fulfills my job passion in the following way: _____
   _____

2. Each of the jobs I'm strongly considering matches my capabilities in the following ways:
   A) _____
   B) _____
   C) _____
   The following is my list of:

   PROS   CONS

   _____   _____
   _____   _____
   _____   _____

3. The pros outweigh the cons in the following ways:
   A) _____
   B) _____
   C) _____

4. How does the job match my top three priorities in terms of what I said I wanted and would accept:
   A) _____
   B) _____
   C) _____

5. The most attractive feature about the job I plan to accept is:
   _____

6. How does the job further/fail to further my career goals?
   A) _____
   B) _____
   C) _____

7. If I stay with this company I can envision myself making career advancements in the
   company within _____ months. I also can see myself moving ahead in terms of title
   and job responsibilities which will include: _____
   _____ within _____ (period of time).

8. The assets I bring to this company include _____ ,
   _____ and _____ .

9. If I take this job, I will stand out in the following ways:
   A) _____
   B) _____
   C) _____

sit in the lobby or walk the hallways, you often see plaques and certificates. Try to notice what lines a company's walls; it will tell you a great deal about how solid they are in their industry and community.

ASSESSING YOUR FUTURE

Make sure the company you choose fits your personal goals. Moving around too much can hurt you in the long run, so as you weigh and balance your choices, ask yourself how long you think you'll stay at that company. Can your long-term goals be met there? Where do you see yourself in a year? Do you want to join the management team one day? As you consider your short- and long-term goals, do some soul-searching. Yes, maybe it is a great company, but is it going where you are? As I said, if you keep "tasting" different jobs, it could come back to bite you. One of the first things I look for when reviewing a resume is to see if the candidate is a job-hopper. I believe that people are consistent; if they've left other jobs within six to nine months, they'll probably do the same to me. Choose wisely so you don't learn at the expense of your image. That's something that will follow you throughout your career. If you're thinking about not listing everything on your resume— and I know some people don't—be careful. At some point a potential employer will find a hole—a six-month period where, work wise, you can't be accounted for. They may think you're hiding something. This can damage your reputation, which is one of the hardest things to re-

store. It's a small world, as I pointed out earlier; people talk, and when they do you want them to say only good things about you. This is one more reason why taking stock of your job offers is vital to your future. Always think ahead.

GOING BACK TO THE BASICS

After you've conferred with a close friend and one or more of your wisest mentors, go back to the basics and put each offer to the test. Examine whether or not the offers you're considering fulfill your passion. See if they match your capabilities and fit within the criteria you've outlined for yourself in terms of what your priorities are. Only then can you make a reasonable decision. Return to your answers in the early worksheets to help clarify the decisions you make.

In addition, the latest worksheet will help you weigh each offer and see if your potential choices match your earlier expectations and projections.

As you review the worksheets in the book's earlier chapters and match those answers with the ones above, you should have a good idea which choice is the most appropriate—i.e., if your answers coincide, you know you're choosing appropriately. If you notice any red flags, such as your passion not being satisfied, your goals not being met, the job responsibilities not being "you," then pass. Take your time and choose wisely. Remember, your life's work will be about networking your way toward your professional heights. Every job you take must help you climb toward that.

chapter fourteen

Feeling Better, Not Bitter

As you conduct your job search, you'll encounter your share of rejection. As hard as it may be at times, you have to muster up your resolve and keep on keepin' on; it's all part of the game. The people who pick themselves up and keep going when it seems the world is against them are the people who ultimately prevail in whatever they choose to undertake. Therein lies the key: the ability to persevere.

If you recall in the introduction to this book, I spoke of three basic necessities you would need to equip yourself with: determination, creativity and perseverance. When you think about it, it's what's gotten you this far in the networking process already. Focusing on that trilogy will continue to keep you tough and unyielding on those difficult days when nothing seems to go your way.

Of the three, I believe that perseverance is the hardest to stick by, but the idea of it should always be at the forefront of your mind.

HANG IN THERE

You probably set out with a strong intent to go after your dream job and got pretty creative in the process. Now the ticket is to keep that intent unwavering—to stay committed to your goal no matter how many times you're rejected.

"N-O—no." We hated to hear that word when we were two, and we still don't like to hear it now. If you're a business professional in any industry, though, it's something you'll hear every day at one time or another. It's not so bad if the "no" is in regard to your company, but when "no" becomes personal—when it's *you* being rejected—it's uncomfortable and often painful.

The trick is not take a "no" personally. Hard to do, I know, but essential to keep you wanting to persevere no matter how frustrated, self-conscious or dejected you get. If we view a rejection as "their loss" or tell ourselves "something better is around the corner," it's easier to take. Remember, an employer is looking for a specific type of person with a package that meets *their* picture, not ours. So "no" has nothing to do with our worth, just what the employer is looking for. Keep your chin up, and know that someone, somewhere wants exactly what you have to offer.

NEVER SAY NEVER

There are many great stories about famous people who were repeatedly told "no" but never gave up. Margaret Mitchell couldn't sell *Gone With the Wind* at first. But after approaching a number of different publishers, she finally won out. In her lengthy pursuit she knew she would have to keep focused on the ultimate goal: seeing her work in print. Mitchell knew part of the game included having to question her worthiness as an author while she plodded through her arduous sales campaign.

The single most important attribute you can possess is an iron will. With it you can accomplish just about anything; without it you may have to rely on luck alone. And we all know how often each of us has won the lottery! A strong will is fertile ground for perseverance, so plant that seed before all else. Remember how you refused to give up as you hunted and gathered your networking base, as you "worked" those contacts for all they were worth? Keep it up. You can't forget about your mission. No matter how many times someone says "no" when you're counting on a "yes," you still need to plow on.

FAMOUS WORDS

Winston Churchill once said, "The definition of power is the ability to go from failure to failure with enthusiasm." I actually have that tacked on my bulletin board. It gives me a kick start when I've run out of resolve.

You, too, can inject yourself with shots of inspiration throughout the day. Like spiritual vitamins, motivational tidbits may be all you need to keep anchored and steadfast. Besides the Winston Churchill remark, I have a list of other proverbs, quotes, quips and anecdotes that give me perspective and persuade me to stay in the game. Most of them are humorous because that approach rearranges my mental closet best of all. My daughter once gave me a bumper sticker that read, "Don't take life so seriously, it's only a temporary situation." The adage about nothing worth anything coming easy often keeps me in the will-to-achieve mode when I want to throw myself face first onto the floor and sob.

Perhaps you have your favorite authors, heroes or mentors who have profoundly affected you with sayings that hit home and continue to stimulate positive thoughts. You want to surround yourself like bubble pack with those uplifting selections. In my interviews with successful business professionals—the ones who had realized their career dreams—they all shared that same habit of collecting inspirational quotes. Each one told me they also kept close famous words from coaches, teachers, therapists and priests, to name but a few. Though their preferences differed, all admitted they also still heard reverbs from their mothers. I tend to believe that "mother's famous words" are the best of all. My own mom had wonderful advice for me. She constantly urged me to ask for what I wanted and to put myself "out there." "The worst anyone can ever say to you is 'no,' honey," she chided. There was something about the way she said this that made "no" seem like less of a rejection.

Whatever reminders you can gather and post nearby is one way to handle the dejection of rejection. Dr. Kappas, to whom I have referred throughout the book, is big on finding positive ways to void out the negatives we encounter every day with the following recipe: For every negative, you need two positives. This, he says, assures that the subconscious mind gives priority to the positives and, in fact, blots out the negative. "It's all a matter of weight," he says. So you, too, can tip the scales in your favor by giving yourself two positive suggestions for every negative circumstance flung at you. For every "no" you hear, find two "yes's" to equal the playing field. I'm trying this out now, and I really like it. It makes me feel like the world is on my side.

Make a list of at least ten of your favorite sayings—the ones that spur you on, especially on those dark days when it seems nothing's going right, whether it's because your networking contacts aren't threading together or your interviewer asked only one question before he showed you to the door. This list will remind you of how capable you are. Continually reviewing such sayings will cause them to seep deeply into your subconscious (a region they tell us doesn't know truth from fiction), and you'll begin to program yourself for only positives.

WHEN THE GOING GETS TOUGH, TAKE TIME OUT

I don't know about you but I've had days when I swear someone was conspiring against me. It just must be the way the stars are aligned or how the universe turns, but there are those days when it seems nothing goes our way and all we hear is "no." In addition to running for your top ten positive affirmations, I also suggest you step outside your own picture and take a break from it all.

Taking time out gives you permission to run away for a period of time; sometimes that's the best thing we can do for ourselves. Rather than fall headlong into a mental downward spiral, stop the plunge by going to recess. That might mean forgetting about the job search or the net-

working probe for the rest of the day and choosing to work on something else productive—that quilt you're making, the car engine you're rebuilding or the novel you started last year. Sometimes a productive distraction is a healthy way to stop, step back and reassemble your perspective. Recess bolsters your resolve and reminds you how vital you really are to the world in which you live. We're all here to do something meaningful, don't forget, but sometimes we lose sight of this, especially when we've had a day or week when rejection is all around us. Working on a project that will provide positive results will reenergize you as you return to your job search.

Many job seekers have told me that hopelessness was hard to fight off when they felt all their attempts were thwarted. Pausing to do something that shows immediate results is one way to stave off the depression that comes with one of those days when nothing seems to go your way.

Write down several projects that provide satisfaction. They can be things you're already in the midst of or things you'd like to do when time permits. Tell yourself you'll resort to them and that it's okay to take time away from the job search or networking when your tolerance for rejection is on overload. You'll accomplish two things: You'll make progress on another endeavor with immediate gratification, and you'll have time to recharge your mental, spiritual and emotional batteries.

REWARD YOURSELF

Even when you feel you have nothing to show for it, hard work is still hard work. It deserves to be rewarded. If you've spent an entire eight-hour day hitting the wall, so to speak, do something special for yourself. I once went through a horrible time close to my birthday, so I threw a surprise birthday party for myself. I sent out invitations detailing the particulars—listing my name in both blanks, "Party for" and "Given by"—asked everyone to arrive at 7:30 p.m., a half hour before I told them I would arrive, and requested that they park down the street so I wouldn't see their cars. The turnout was great. I feigned total surprise and they all went along with it. I felt most proud that I had taken full responsibility for doing something to reward myself during a trying time.

Going shopping for awhile, making yourself your favorite cake, taking in a movie or picking up a new music CD are wonderful ways to say to yourself: "You're special, and I think you're important, so don't give up. You'll make it!"

Once again, compose a creative list of personal rewards—small to big—that would amuse you and assuage your frustrated and hurt feelings. No one knows better than you what you want!

I now make it a habit to give myself a gift (it can even be a chocolate bar) when I've put a great deal of effort into anything, fruitless or not. One note of caution: Try not to reward yourself with things like too many sweets, splurging too much at the mall or other things that might get you into trouble. The idea with this reward system is to congratulate yourself with random acts of kindness for efforts well expended. It's not only OK, but absolutely necessary, to remind yourself that you're unique and special and your hard work has not gone unnoticed. Most of all, such a regular exercise provides balance. Just watch the excesses.

Another idea you may want to capitalize on: Dr. Kappas has a book he uses for his patients whereby they are asked to keep a mental bank. They write down a reasonable dollar amount as compensation for their efforts. For instance, if they're in sales and didn't sell anything one day but made fourteen sales calls, they're instructed to record a dollar amount they paid to themselves as a symbol of remuneration for their hard work. Kappas swears this record keeping will ultimately cause real rewards to materialize. You may want to try this. It can make you feel very rich at the end of any day, even a day filled with rejection. It's just one more way to come upon a glimmer of inspiration.

I'LL SHOW YOU AND ME, AND THE REST OF THE WORLD, TOO

One of the greatest motivators in the world can be rejection. I often get inspired when someone tells me "no." I react inwardly with anger, but rather than let it fester, I use it as fuel to launch me into action to make something positive happen. I refuse to be down for long, and if I get a "no" when I was expecting "yes," it makes me try even harder. I become compelled to show them and me, and the rest of the world, that I can—whatever "I can" is, at the moment. When you have a great deal of personal pride, a rejection can actually be a wonderful catalyst to get you off your duff and make "it" happen. So let your reaction to your rejection culminate in positive results. When you can convert negative energy into positive, you are as powerful as you can possibly be. Fear and anger can be great mental stimuli in punting you forward to reach your goals. As primal as these emotions are, we definitely feel them when we have been rejected. The trick is to use these emotions in a positive, constructive way. In all candor, most of my major accomplishments have come as a result of someone either flatly saying, "You can't do that," or implying it indirectly through some type of rejection like: "If we do decide to use your services, we'll let you know." Subtle, yes, but still real rejection.

Many great artists, inventors and entrepreneurs managed greatness out of a manic reaction to rejection. One example I read about is Fredrick Smith, the man who started Federal Express. His billion-dollar company was a result of someone scoffing at his idea. While attending business school, Smith wrote a thesis on how his suggested operation would work. As the story goes, his professor laughingly flunked him. "Impossible," was the teacher's reaction; no one could deposit all packages in one location, then reroute them overnight to other sites. Well, I don't have to tell you how successful this company has become. One of Smith's adages may have been "He who laughs last, laughs best." I'm sure he's still doing that, all the way to the bank.

This is going to be a strange homework assignment, but I'm going to ask you to do it anyway. Research at least six people, either current or in history, who were told "no" yet went on to become huge successes because their rejection spurred them on. Study their case histories, and listen carefully to what they had to say about their climb to success and what they did to keep themselves inspired. This will be a big help since most of us find our inspiration from other people, not things. I'll give you one hint for starters: Watch the *Biography* series on the Arts and Entertainment channel. The common denominator with many of these hugely successful personalities is that someone along the way told them "no," which fired them up, big time. Van Gogh was ridiculed for his work, Buckminster Fuller was reminded he didn't have a college diploma, Harrison Ford was told he didn't have the looks to be a leading man and Howard Hughes was told he would never get his Spruce Goose off the

ground. These are only a handful of people who wouldn't take "no" for an answer. Not only would they not accept the negative, they continued to uphold the positive—to prove they were not simply a one-time fluke. Again, a common trait was perseverance in the face of adversity. These were all people who allowed the notion of rejection to influence them positively. Make your list of interesting people who did it "their way." They're all around you. They don't have to be famous people in history; many of them may live next door. Give great attention to the factors that inspired these people. I guarantee you, each of them had inspirational sources they tapped into to keep them moving forward.

GIVING IT YOUR ALL TO GET TO YOUR BEST

Most of us don't use near our full potential until we've hit bottom. A friend of mine, Louis Sabatasso, owner of one of the country's largest pizza manufacturing companies, started with two hundred dollars and a small storefront facility making pizza shells. He had a number of people say "no" when he tried to borrow money to grow his business. He told me once that every time someone said "no," he dug deep and found determination within himself. "I truly don't believe anyone in the world of business can possibly demonstrate their full potential without rejection," he said during a lecture, "for it is when each of us is faced with adversity that we have no alternative but to resort to our greatest personal potential and power." Louis ultimately sold his business for twenty million.

LOOKING FORWARD TO LOOKING AHEAD

Another way to maintain a good measure of inspiration through the mire of rejection is to keep your eye on the future. Realize that you have a definite goal in mind, and like climbing a mountain, allow yourself a slip or two as you head for the top. When you look to where you're aiming your career, you keep a healthier perspective overall. Sometimes the wall of rejection can make us feel trapped and helpless, yet when we look to what lies ahead, we renew our deepest sense of determination.

A close girlfriend of mine found herself divorced at twenty-seven with three small daughters. She desperately wanted to go to law school and become a lawyer. The steps along the way were arduous: She had to work full-time, care for her children and scrape the money together to go to law school. It took her more than three years, but she did it. In her lectures about her success as an attorney, she says it was all due to her ability to keep her eye on the future and the ultimate reward for her hard work. She meditated on it every day, she told a group of first-year law students. So while it seemed like the world was saying "no" to her (in a more subtle way), she didn't let it deter her from her final goal.

Rejection can come from many directions. The idea is to keep your eye toward your future.

WHAT TO DO WHEN YOU GET THOSE NEGATIVE FEELINGS

What about those horrible feelings only a rejection can invoke? Always remember: They are only temporary. Another of my favorite mom adages is: "This too shall pass." I recite that to myself whenever I get the blues as a result of a "no." I realize I won't feel down for long or forever. But there are moments when we need to take pause and acknowledge that we do feel bad, and it's okay to do so.

Dr. Kappas has a wonderful way of coaching his patients through rejection. He asks them to decide how long they wish to spend wallowing in their hurt feelings. They decide if it's ten minutes, ten hours, a full week—then Kappas asks them to keep track of this allotment of time with their watch. When their time is up, it's up, and they have to promise to move on. There is something wonderful about allowing ourselves the time to roll around in the sadness until those feelings dissipate. It precludes us from hanging onto such negative energy by not forcing ourselves to resist it. We don't want to carry our insecure feelings to the next appointment, so wallow in it, then release it. I have a friend who calls her wallow time her "bathrobe day." She simply puts her robe on—no makeup, no hairdo—and stays in it. She feels sorry for herself for a whole day. She feels great the next day because she didn't neglect those feelings that were all too real.

After brushing myself off from "rolling around in it," I put my chin up and refocus on the future and the rewards I will one day claim as a result of my hard work and efforts.

Don't feel guilty about making a fuss over being rejected. Your ability to agonize for awhile could be one more way to inspire yourself to get up and go again.

ADDING UP THE POSITIVES TO ELIMINATE YOUR NEGATIVES

Let's recap the different ways you can reunite yourself with inspiration when faced with rejection:

1. Make a list of your top ten (or more if you like) favorite positive affirmations. They can be those tidbits passed on by your coach, favorite teacher, therapist or godparent. Most of all, record those wonderful pearls of wisdom your

mother told you. Keep them posted in front of you or within close reach.

2. For every negative, give yourself two positives. Write these down if you care to. Keeping a journal is a great way to remind yourself of all you really are and to refresh your memory about the truth when your perspective goes to hell.

3. Make a list of what you can do when you take a time-out. What other productive projects could you putter with that will reignite your sense of inspiration?

4. Reward yourself. What can you give yourself on a difficult day that would say "thanks for all the hard work"? These don't have to be large gifts, just things that perk you up and make you feel special.

5. Play the mental-bank game. Pay yourself a symbolic sum of money for all your efforts, even if they resulted in a rejection. Your efforts are still worth something.

6. Ask yourself if you're motivated by fear and anger. If the answer is "yes," describe to what lengths you will go—and how—to show "them" and "you" that you really can achieve great heights.

7. Keep track of what new and wonderful attributes you notice about yourself when the chips are down. What have you pulled from deep inside that inspired you again, despite your disappointment?

8. Look ahead. Sometimes it's hard, but keep your eye on the bigger picture and your ultimate goal. This should make the "big" rejection seem like just a small bump in the road on your way to that final destination. Keep a keen awareness of what that end result will mean in the long run.

Remember that everyone, no matter how successful or wealthy or accomplished they are, has bad days. Each of us has times when we have to face rejection; it's part of the human condition. But those times when we feel less than worthy or even hopeless are only temporary feelings. Everything will change. As Scarlett O'Hara remarked: "Tomorrow is another day." Don't ever lose sight of the bigger picture. It's that resolve that keeps us steady. Do whatever it takes for you to pick yourself up, dust yourself off and start all over again.

Are We There Yet?

chapter fifteen

Let's assume you've worked diligently at all the lessons in the previous chapters, and because of the positive and plentiful results you've produced, you have successfully amassed a healthy and substantial networking base. I'm also assuming by now that you've either landed the job you wanted, or you're well on your way to making that happen. In any case, the next step is to learn how to stay in the networking loop and have it work for you.

WHAT A PLAN

Once you've clarified your goals, you can lay out a practical plan that addresses who you're going to network with and through what means. Are you going to vow to attend two industry-related functions per month? Join one new group a year? Investigate what new and exciting associations match your career interests? Plan ahead as you set your goals. You don't want to spin in a networking circle, getting nowhere.

The other type of plan I consider a must is a business plan—for yourself! This plan should include all the particulars you would see in any company business plan. For starters, you need some kind of vision statement. For those of you not familiar with that term, a vision or mission statement is a brief, simple paragraph that clearly states your position, i.e., who you are and what you're up to. The following is an example:

As a professional speech therapist, I am dedicated to assisting a variety of individuals with their speech impediments and inadequacies to help them gain confidence and comfort as they go about their daily verbal communication tasks.

Actually, most vision statements serve as a preamble to a business plan—to set the tone. Business plans are in vogue whether we're talking about individuals or corporations. Your career requires a business plan, so if you're an entrepreneur or an employee for a large company, you're smart to take the time it requires to devise one.

Most people don't think of themselves in

terms of being an "entity" but I'm asking you to do so. And as you do, keep in mind that a business plan charts projections for both short- and long-term goals. I'm not suggesting you'll need some formal, spiral-bound document, so don't get carried away. All you really need is something simple: a couple of pages you can keep with all your other files and records. This, too, you will continually monitor.

The following is a shorthand version of a business plan that you can use as a guideline to devise your own. Again, theoretically, it follows the same format as that which is used for major corporations:

Business Plan for
AMANDA K. MANLEY
Speech Therapist

PAGE ONE:

Vision Statement: (same as above)

PAGE TWO:

Objective:
To build a strong practice and gain substantial experience in the field of speech therapy so I will be in a position to open my own speech therapy clinic in no later than five years from today's date.

PAGE THREE:

Projections:
Year one:
- Build a practice of 250 patients that meet with me monthly.
- Earn $32,000 per year.
- Add to my skills by taking at least two classes and studying subject matter four hours weekly to increase my level of knowledge.
- Begin to take business classes that will prepare me to open my own business.

Year two:
- Increase my client base by 15 percent.
- Earn $36,000 a year.
- Increase skill level by taking continuing education so I can upgrade my certification to certified speech therapist.
- Seek out and study similar businesses to that which I plan to open.

Year three:
- Increase my client base by 15 percent.
- Earn $40,000 a year.
- Take classes that further educate me in the field of speech therapy, and enroll in a business school to study accounting and business management.
- Connect with two mentors, both of whom have strong business experience and are successful in their fields.

Year four:
- Increase client base by an additional 10 percent.
- Earn $43,000 a year.
- Take additional business classes that focus on growth and expansion.
- Begin to solicit an advisory board of directors to guide and direct me.
- Raise $75,000 to capitalize my business venture.
- Design my marketing plan.
- Begin to look for a facility.

Year five:
- Put marketing plan into action.
- Earn $60,000 per year.
- Open my own clinic!!!

As you can see, you'll eventually want to put together a marketing plan, i.e., a detailed account of how you will go about selling yourself.

Will it be through direct mail, advertising and public relations? Whether you have your own company or plan to work for a large conglomerate, you should employ all the aforementioned to promote yourself. Ultimately, *you* are the product! In addition to what I've just mentioned, what other means would be available to you to sell yourself? Yes, you have your package, which you worked on earlier, but that's a little different. You prepared that to introduce yourself. Granted, it too should be designed to "sell" you, but you need a plan to go with it.

As you think along additional lines of preparing that "corporate" plan, also think about assembling a board of directors just like a CEO would do—a group of advisors and mentors who can help you reach your goals and offer advice and guidance as you move forward. Next, you'll need an operating budget for yourself. Projections beyond the first five years are also important. My advisors suggest a ten-year plan. Also, think about a clear definition of your product line, whether it's a service or tangible goods. Though it may sound strange, you need to issue quarterly and annual reports. These should include earnings reports, expenditures, profit-and-loss statements and a recap of the year's accomplishments. If you prepare these, you will get a strong, objective picture of where you are and where you're going.

Once again, you don't need to have your own company to have a business plan nor do you need to produce a product. When you prepare a personal business plan *you* are the company and the product!

DO YOU KNOW WHERE YOU'RE GOING?

The heads of several executive search firms said those who have a personal business plan tend to be far more successful than those who don't. The single most important reason why, they all said conclusively, was because that person knew what she wanted and therefore found it was easier to network her way to where she was going. "You can't get to the finish line if you don't know where it is," one laughed.

So before you work that loop, you want to work the plan. The most exciting aspect of this business plan is that you can network your way into and around it. It will take others to help you clarify goals, set a course and keep on it all through your professional life. How you put your networking database together and how you continue to use it has a great deal to do with your ability to make a concrete plan that will give you people to contact for help and the drive to stay in the loop. If you immerse yourself in the thick of the loop, all things are possible.

As you go about your networking tasks, match your activities against what you've laid out for yourself in your personalized business plan and see if, in fact, you're making the progress you had mapped out in your earlier projections. Determine whether or not you're staying the course of your mission or vision statement. Most of us have some general sense of our success as time passes, but to see it in black and white and check on it regularly, is a more effective method for keeping us on track and measuring our progress. So make a clear-cut business plan that coincides with your expectations. Attention to this detail has a great deal to do with the amount of control you will maintain over your career in the years that lie ahead.

GREAT EXPECTATIONS

With your business plan in front of you, ask yourself what you expect from your networking efforts. Are you considering the possibility of making a career change at some point down the line? Do you want to network to keep your professional/social life going? Are you looking for new clients from such activity? Are you hoping to hob-knob with the powers that be? Before you continue to network, clarify your reason for doing it. Have a heart-to-heart with yourself on just what it is you expect to gain. I know people who aimlessly hop from mixer to mixer, not knowing why they're doing it. They show up because they think they should. Set forth some concrete goals, purpose or purposes, always keeping in mind the objectives set forth in your business plan.

There is really no one right answer for why it is you will continue to network. Making clear decisions on what you expect from doing it, though, will help move you forward, as well as provide you with a sense of satisfaction that your time and efforts are being well spent.

HOW WILL YOUR GARDEN GROW?

Think of your networking database like a garden; it needs regular planting and harvesting and, in between, lots of care. There is no such thing as completion. You're regularly maintaining and adding to it, watching it grow.

Once you've established what you hope to accomplish by networking, decide exactly how you will feed and care for your networking database. Will you, for instance, look in on it once a week? Once a month? You have to understand what it will take—in terms of your personal needs—to keep your network bank growing and bountiful.

Review the status of your contact list no less than once quarterly. Whatever way you organized and delineated your database, you'll want to go back and make changes. Are there deletions you need to make? Have you made new contacts, met new people or heard of others you

want to stay in touch with or who can help you in your professional job search or with the progression of your career? Resolve to add names and sources to your lists at least once monthly. If you become lax, your list will slowly deteriorate; many of the contacts you've collected may move away, fade away or possibly even pass away. Staying on top of changes is essential. I know of people who have worked for an entire year diligently building a networking database, then quit. They thought their work was done, but like any collection, there is never an end to the gathering process. When it comes to your networking upkeep, gathering information will come in two forms: either updating existing file entries or making new additions.

Focus your attention on whatever changes affect the people and resources for which you have files. It's important then to set up an accessible system—a self-designed, disciplined, personal program, that will keep your networking archives current and meaningful. Here's one way to measure the power of what you've collected: If someone was in direct competition with you, would they benefit greatly from having your networking files? If not, you know you've got work to do. If so, then it's probably because you've taken good care of those files, and they're thorough and up to date.

MEET AND GREET

Now that you've carefully prepared "the plan," it's time to make a file tabbed "commitments." This should include a list of places, dates and times of meetings and events you plan to attend for at least a three-month period. Such activities should be germane to your professional pursuits. Keep any literature on the organizations that host these events—newsletters, brochures, membership rosters, newspaper articles—any collateral materials that will keep you informed about who they are, what their purpose is and what they can offer. You can easily add to this commitment file as you proceed through any year. Warning: Don't make so many commitments to attend events and meetings that the rest of your life begins to suffer. (In fact, part of your personal business plan should include personal goals for yourself, too, i.e., joining a gym, taking x-amount of vacation time, etc.)

One source told me that attending one event per week—a lecture, chamber mixer, dinner meeting—was more than adequate to stay in the loop. Most industry organizations meet once monthly, so it would not be impossible to be active in four associations. Another source told me she belonged to twenty-five groups and rotated her appearances at their scheduled events. She agreed that she was only able to attend two functions per year, though she was a registered member for several, but this arrangement worked for her.

I'm pushing this commitment program because in my experience, it's the most reasonable way to stay in the loop. I can honestly say that I have yet to attend a meeting or function where someone hasn't told me about another event that interests me. It's easy to get tied up in the daily tasks of your job (not to mention the needs of your personal life) and drop out for a time. But as a networker, there is no vacation. Most business opportunities come from meeting and greeting other people in the business world, so each of us has to get and stay involved in something industry related. I can't stress this enough for those of you looking to move beyond your current horizons. Think about it: How many business professionals do you know who stay status quo? Not too many for too long.

Get involved but in an organized way. Pull out your daily planner—whatever form you prefer—and mark those dates and times you're going to set aside for meeting and greeting.

GET OUT OF TOWN

Another terrific way to work the loop is to get out of town. Look for a learning opportunity or an industry get-together that takes you from your daily habitat to a hotel or resort facility once a year for a few days. I can't think of one industry—from religion to accounting—that doesn't offer some seminar or recreational event that benefits those in its field.

There is something stimulating about a business retreat. You're totally focused on the subject at hand. When you're out of town with other business pros you're not thinking about what you need to remember at the grocery store, or whether you have time to stop at the cleaners on your way to the parent-teacher's conference. You're where you are to do something specific and well planned.

I mentioned earlier that I study the vast world of improvisational comedy since I've taught it for thirty years. I need and want something new constantly. Though I had never done something like it before, I signed up for a seven-day improv workshop in Monterey, California, to study with a handful of the country's leading instructors. One had been a guiding force and instructor for award-winning actress Helen Hunt, while another had been a cast member with John Belushi, Gilda Radner, Bill Murray, John Candy and others at Second City in Chicago. While his teammates went on to *Saturday Night Live* and other showbiz activities, my teacher continued to instruct and direct. This week he was mine! Although I was reluctant at first to enroll in this workshop because of too much time away from work, I went anyway. It turned out to be a life-changing event and one of the most significant weeks of my entire life. It was the initial inspiration for me to finally write and star in my own one-woman show, which I had put off for twenty-seven years.

Even more meaningful, I met at least sixty new people, but unlike one of those one-evening industry events, I had time to really get to know many of them. We attended classes together, ate three meals a day in one another's company and chatted around the fireplace as the evenings wound down. I spent the entire week learning, honing my skills, getting appreciation for my talent and getting to know these people as individuals. We shared stories, laughs, even a few tears. I made a handful of dear friends from that experience. We vowed to stay in touch and we have. Through these contacts, I continue to have business sent my way. Since they were from all over the country, I have gladly sent them referrals as well.

Going off for a few days to a week is similar to summer camp. It's just that the kids are bigger. People seem to let down their professional guard in that setting. There is something about the camaraderie that exists away from home that's just a little different than when we attend events for an hour or two in our own safe environment. My theory is we are all so busy and preoccupied with what surrounds us that we can't slow down long enough to really delve into the "people thing." We meet and greet, and that's all well and fine. But do those functions offer the same opportunities as when we're corralled in the same place with the same people for a length of time? I don't think they can. And what irony: We attend our local events for just that reason—to make friends and contacts. I urge you to sign up for at least one out-of-town event per year—one that will aid in your career

pursuits and afford you the opportunity to make lasting relationships.

Whether your interactions with others are through short- or long-term events, remember it's all about relationships. Make the most of every one of them.

UNFORGETTABLE

I remarked earlier that most of us have an urge to move beyond where we've been before; no more is that apparent than in the area of a career. If we look around, most of us know very few people who are in the same job they were in five, ten and twenty years ago. Most people climb higher or expand outward—that's the law of the workplace universe.

Keeping your antenna tuned to what opportunities may be in the offing is vital to your career growth, and staying in touch with those who can give you the jobs you want as you climb the professional ladder is equally as important.

Here's the problem: Each of us meets so many people every day that it is easy to forget faces and names. It is up to you as an ardent networker to find ways to stay memorable to those who can help you get ahead. Reach out to those you want to stay in front of—to keep showing up in one way or another—to make the kind of impression that will make them want to remember you. XYZ Company may not have an opening today, but how about six months from now? Or maybe they know someone who could use your services or talent. They just might refer someone to *you*.

This bears repeating: Keep careful records of company presidents, human resource directors and all others who do the hiring, so you can remind them in clever and constant ways that you exist and would be an asset to their organization.

GETTING PERSONAL AND STAYING LINKED

I have one business associate who has a file she has titled "Heavy Hitters." She keeps updated records of pertinent information like names and profiles of people in her industry. She's a stockbroker and is militant about staying in touch with every important contact she's ever come upon. She sends them a personal note, newspaper clippings about herself (she's active in several organizations and has been featured in their newsletters and local papers) and articles she thinks they may find of interest, at least once every three to six months. She's the business associate I referred to earlier who has learned the date of each important person's birthday and sends him or her a card and a personal note. To receive a card from someone I hardly know is a real treat. People we make feel important are more apt to take our calls and want to help us with whatever we need, be it a networking contact or a job.

It's always about making a good impression when it comes to the business world, not only to the people you want to buy your services, provide a networking contact or hire you, but also individuals who have shown genuine interest in who you are, what you do and where you're going.

I have many business associates but one in particular has become intrigued with what I do. I make a point to stay in touch with her for various reasons. I may call to let her know I'm looking for additional speaking engagements; she may be the first person I alert to a new class I'm offering, or I sometimes just bring her up to speed on news about mutual friends. Maybe you have a special friend who is really interested in you and the work you do. My friend is always on the lookout for me—letting me know about new opportunities, putting me in touch with a company who may need my services. But you must contact these special few regularly. Don't say "I'll call tomorrow"—a whole year can go by and you still haven't called!

MAYDAY ANY DAY

Let members of the professional community stay aware of what you need and want from one another. How can anyone help you if they don't know what it is you need? We all get caught up in our daily minutiae, and we don't realize someone needs our help, advice or a contact, unless we hear from them. Similarly, they don't know we need them unless they hear from us.

Make your needs known to friends and business colleagues alike. Communicating can't only be done through ESP! You have to pick up the phone or show up at the next industry function and put your requests out there. Networking with friends and business associates with whom you are most comfortable is probably a big portion of your networking base, so your ability to stay active with them strengthens the core of your almighty loop. Opening communication with them as well as all the new people you will come upon is crucial. Overall, how can you make this happen? Devote a certain amount of your work schedule to checking in with pals and colleagues.

How can you stay memorable to the other people you need? Be creative with your ideas. Don't be patronizing or imposing. Keep accurate records and update them. Stay in touch or do whatever it takes to connect regularly. They are a big part of your loop.

TRADING PLACES

Another suggestion for staying active as a networker is to find yourself a trusted networking buddy. Find someone who has similar professional needs. Agree to swap networking contacts at a semiyearly lunch meeting. (You can do this more frequently if you like.) You bring your list; she brings hers. Each of you doubles your contacts and shares information you may never have come upon otherwise. Remember all the effort you put into compiling your list in the first place. Your buddy probably did the same. When you consider the amount of time spent, there's a great deal of value to be derived from what you've amassed.

If you really want to be industrious, do what one of my friends did. He started a networking club, called APEX, within his professional community. At monthly breakfast meetings, each person is required to bring at least one new member, and each is also responsible for sharing his or her contacts. The rule is that there can only be one of whatever profession in the group. For instance: one attorney, one banker, one cellular telephone salesperson, one corporate human resource trainer, etc. At every meeting different people stand and thank so-and-so for the such-and-such lead that led to new business. My friend faxes a tally of the dollar amount of business done each month by the group as a total, and the numbers are astounding. Their whole purpose for meeting is to create new networking opportunities. Even their guest speakers are handpicked so they can shed light on the subject of networking.

There are, of course, other groups across the country, in small towns and big cities, who meet for nothing more than to aid people in the "looping" process.

You may want to start a similar group among your business colleagues, whether you're all from different industries or in the same field. The focus should always be on networking;

you'll stay in the loop by just showing up.

If this concept doesn't appeal to you, that's fine, but see what other creative ideas you can think up that would accomplish similar goals. (There may be some unique approach to establishing other networking loops with those around you.) Get together with other innovators—people with like minds— and brainstorm. Ask around, too. People may have ideas you can borrow that will help you focus on creating mini-loops.

WHATEVER WORKS, DO IT

As you journey along your own networking path, see what works for you. We're all different in what feels right and what is appropriate to our respective careers. There is no one right way of staying in the loop. Devise as many ways for staying active as are practical. Don't forget to keep track of your results. Reviewing what seems to move you forward and ahead is vital. As busy as you are, don't waste valuable time networking with people who don't share similar interests or lack your drive and enthusiasm.

Stick to whatever game plan keeps you networking on a regular basis. There is no such thing as doing a big blast of networking then letting go. It is something you must keep after for the rest of your professional life if you expect to expand and grow. I have no patience for people who complain that they have little time to network; that it takes too much effort; that they have no energy after handling the responsibilities of their respective jobs. I say phooey! Each of us has to make the time. One of my mentors told me that he allocated 10 percent of his time every day to networking in some form or another. It was always at the forefront of his thinking. You should make it part of your daily agenda, too. With all this in mind, don't let up

WORKSHEET: NETWORKING TO THE FUTURE AND WORKING THE LOOP

1. How will your garden grow? What methods will you employ to keep your networking database up to date? What about adding to it?

   My plan for keeping files and records up to date is to do the following:

   A) _____

   B) _____

   C) _____

   D) _____

   E) _____

   I plan to do this assignment every _____ months.

2. What are your expectations for working your networking loop? Clarify your reasons for doing it. Are you just hanging out or are you looking for new career opportunities, friends in the business community, clients?

   My expectations from staying in the networking loop and working it are as follows:

   A) _____

   B) _____

   C) _____

   D) _____

   E) _____

3. To keep working the loop I plan to belong to _____ groups.

4. The following is a list of those organizations and associations I will join in addition to those which I already belong:

   A) _____

   B) _____

   C) _____

   D) _____

   E) _____

5. I will attend functions sponsored by these groups every _____ month.

6. My vision statement regarding who I am and where I'm going is:

   _____

   _____

   _____

   _____

continued

7. With regard to a business plan and my future as a business professional, the following represents my five-year business plan strategy:

_____

_____

_____

_____

_____

8. Five out-of-town events I can participate in to broaden my networking horizons:

A) _____

B) _____

C) _____

D) _____

E) _____

9. The following are a handful of ways I will continually put myself before others to remind them of my goals and interests:

A) _____

B) _____

C) _____

D) _____

E) _____

10. Individuals I will put myself before on a *regular* basis so they are kept abreast of my networking needs:

A) _____

B) _____

C) _____

D) _____

E) _____

11. Friends and business associates I will contact *occasionally* to let them know what I need and where I'm going with my career:

A) _____

B) _____

C) _____

D) _____

E) _____

continued

12. Who I might contact to trade networking lists with:

A) _____

B) _____

C) _____

D) _____

E) _____

13. Individuals with similar interests who I can contact to start a club or group:

A) _____

B) _____

C) _____

D) _____

E) _____

14. The following represents a handful of clever and unique ways I can start and/or join with others in starting a networking club:

A) _____

B) _____

C) _____

D) _____

E) _____

15. I'll contact:

A) _____

B) _____

C) _____

D) _____

E) _____

16. The guidelines and innovative ideas we can implement to make such a club successful:

A) _____

B) _____

C) _____

D) _____

E) _____

My suggestions for what we can call such a club:

_____

17. Even though I provided a slew of creative suggestions for staying in the loop, make a list of at least ten of your own creative and different ideas not discussed that could help you stay in the networking loop and work it.

_____   _____

_____   _____

_____   _____

_____   _____

_____   _____

on your networking follow-through tasks. You've already done the groundwork, and you've learned how to play the networking game well. Continuing the process should be easy.

Whatever methods you choose to stay in the loop, make them fun and pleasurable. None of us want to do something we don't enjoy for very long. Choose carefully. Look at networking as one of the pluses to being a working professional. It can be one of the most interesting and profitable ways of spending time as you build and nurture your career. More importantly, networking is all about people. Nothing is more valuable than relationships.

chapter sixteen

Bibliography for the Ardent Networker

I mentioned in chapter five that reference books are vital for keeping up with what is happening in the world of networking. As changes occur (and they constantly will in the business world) you want to keep abreast of new and interesting ways to network. That being the case, it's important to read. Granted, you can plug into the Internet; (there's lots of good information there), but I can't stress enough how helpful it is having your own library. How-to books have become popular staples in the past two decades. I don't know anyone who hasn't read some type of how-to. Experts tells us an influx of these books will become even more prevalent as we turn the corner to the next century. Books will never go out of style.

Though it's unrealistic to go out and buy every self-help-in-the-business-world book, you can gradually accumulate a substantial shelf or two of texts and manuals that will serve as great reference material—information you can read now and later leaf through as you build your career.

In addition to reference books, you should collect reading materials that will keep you current—books that fall in the instant-hit category, such as *The One Minute Manager*. These books give you a distinct feel for what is currently happening in the world of business, or even more importantly, where it is going. As a networker you want to stay up with—if not two beats ahead of—what's going on at all times. I especially like these books because they challenge my existing skill level in some way and motivate me to make positive changes.

The following list of books fall into seven categories: Networking Guides, Communication, Public Speaking, Organization, Careers, Motivation, Etiquette. They will give you a good start as you begin your networking trek.

NETWORKING GUIDES

Career Advancement Networking, Winthrop W. Hamilton

Fifty-Two Ways to Reconnect, Follow-Up and Stay in Touch: When You Don't Have Time to Network, Anne Baber and Lynne Waymon

Great Connections: Small Talk and Networking for Businesspeople, Anne Baber and Lynne Waymon

How to Work a Room: Learn the Strategies of Savvy Socializing for Business and Personal Success, Susan Roane

Interactive Interfaces and Human Networks, Ranulph Glanville and Gerard De Zeeuw, ed.

It's Who You Know: Career Strategies for Making Effective Personal Contacts, Cynthia Chin-Lee

National Business Employment Weekly Networking, Douglas B. Richardson

Networking With the Affluent and Their Advisors, Thomas J. Stanley

Networking: Building Relationships, Building Success, Kevin J. Cashman, Paul L. Cimmerer and James W. Lewis.

Networking: How to Creatively Tap Your People Resources, Colleen S. Clarke

Networking Smart: How to Build Relationships for Personal and Organizational Success, Wayne E. Baker

Networking Success: How to Turn Business and Financial Relationships Into Fun and Profit, Anne Boe

Networks and Organizations: Structure, Form and Action, ed. by Nitin Nohria and Robert G. Eccles

People Power: How to Create a Lifetime Network for Business, Career and Personal Advancement, Donna Fisher

Richard Beatty's Job Search Networking, Richard H. Beatty

The Secrets of Savvy Networking: How to Make the Best Connections for Business and Personal Success, Susan Roane

COMMUNICATION

Between People: Communicating One-to-One, John A. Sanford

Conversation Made Easy, Elliot Russell

Conversationally Speaking: Tested New Ways to Increase Your Personal and Social Effectiveness, Alan Garner

Coping With Difficult People, Robert M. Bramson

He Says, She Says: Closing the Communication Gap Between the Sexes, Lillian Glass

How to Start a Conversation and Make Friends, Doug Gabor

How to Turn an Interview Into a Job, Jeffrey G. Allen

How to Win Friends and Influence People, Dale Carnegie

Killer Interviews, Frederick W. Ball and Barbara B. Ball

Lifetime Conversation Guide, James K. Van Fleet

Making People Talk, Barry Farber

101 Dynamite Answers to Interview Questions: No More Sweaty Palms, Caryl Rae Krannich and Ronald L. Krannich

Say It With Power and Confidence, Patrick J. Collins

Social Organizations: Interaction Inside, Outside and Between Organizations, Goran Ahrne

When I Say This, Do You Mean That . . . ? One-On-One Skills for the Business Professional, Cherie Kerr

PUBLIC SPEAKING

The Art of Breathing, Nancy Zi

The Elements of Speechwriting and Public Speaking, Jeff Scott Cook

How to Say It: Choice Words, Phrases, Sentences and Paragraphs for Every Situation, Rosalie Maggio

How to Write, Speak, and Think More Effectively, Rudolf Flesch

I Can See You Naked: A New Revised Edition of

the National Bestseller on Making Fearless Presentations, Ron Hoff

I've Asked Miller to Say a Few Words: New and Exciting Ways to Improve Speaking and Presentation Skills Through the Use of Improvisational Comedy Techniques, Cherie Kerr

The Power of Public Speaking, Marie Stuttard

Say It With Confidence: Overcome the Mental Blocks That Keep You From Making Great Presentations and Speeches, Margo T. Krasne

Smart Speaking: Sixty-Second Strategies for More Than 100 Speaking Problems and Fears, Laurie Schloff and Marcia Yudkin

Speak With Power and Grace: A Woman's Guide to Public Speaking, Linda D. Swink

ORGANIZATION

The Administrative Assistant, Brenda Bailey-Hughes

Adminstrative Assistant's and Secretary's Handbook, J. Stroman and K. Wilson

The Art of the Long View: Planning for the Future in an Uncertain World, Peter Schwartz

Assessment for Decision, edited by Donald R. Peterson and Daniel B. Fishman

Design of Office Information Systems, C.A. Ellis and N. Naffah

The Discipline of Market Leaders: Choose Your Customers, Narrow Your Focus, Dominate Your Market, Michael Treacy and Fred Wiersema

The End of Bureaucracy and the Rise of the Intelligent Organization, Gifford and Elizabeth Pinchot

Megatrends: Ten New Directions Transforming Our Lives, John Naisbitt

The Office Sourcebook, Mary A. De Vries

100 Things to Always Remember—and One Thing to Never Forget, Alin Austin

The One Minute Manager, Kenneth Blanchard and Spencer Johnson

Organizational Troubleshooting: Asking the Right Questions, Finding the Right Answers, Reed E. Nelson

Strategic Planning: What Every Manager Must Know, George A. Steiner

365 Ways to Simplify Your Work Life: Ideas That Bring More Time, Freedom and Satisfaction to Daily Work, Odette Pollar

Thriving On Chaos: Handbook for a Management Revolution, Tom Peters

201 Ways to Manage Your Time Better, Alan Axelrod

CAREERS

Career Smarts: Jobs With a Future, Martin Yate

The Directory of Executive Recruiters, Kennedy Information LLC

Do What You Are: Discover the Perfect Career for You Through the Secrets of Personality Type, Paul D. Tieger and Barbara Barron-Tieger

Finding Your Perfect Work: The New Career Guide to Making a Living, Creating a Life, Paul and Sarah Edwards

Get Ahead, Stay Ahead: Learn the 70 Most Important Career Skills, Traits and Attitudes to Stay Employed, Get Promoted, Get a Better Job, Dianna Booher

Losing Your Job—Reclaiming Your Soul: Stories of Resilience, Renewal and Hope, Mary Lynn Pulley

Making Career Transitions, Jane Ballback and Jan Slater

100 Best Careers for the Twenty-First Century, Shelly Field

Personal Best: 1001 Great Ideas for Achieving Success in Your Career, Joe Tye with *National Business Employment Weekly*

What Color Is Your Parachute? Richard Nelson
 Bolles

MOTIVATION

The Celestine Prophecy, James Redfield
Chicken Soup for the Soul, Jack Canfield and
 Mark Victor Hansen
*Don't Sweat the Small Stuff—and It's All Small
 Stuff*, Richard Carlson
*Don't Worry, Make Money: Spiritual and
 Practical Ways to Create Abundance and More
 Fun in Your Life*, Richard Carlson
*Do What You Love, the Money Will Follow:
 Discovering Your Right Livelihood*, Marsha
 Sinetar
Feeling Good: The New Mood Therapy, David D.
 Burns
Fire in the Belly: On Being a Man, Sam Keen
*14,000 Things to Be Happy About: The Happy
 Book*, Barbara Kipfer
*How High Can You Bounce? Turn Your Setbacks
 Into Comebacks*, Roger Crawford
Learned Optimism, Martin E.P. Seligman
The Little Engine That Could, Watty Piper
*Napoleon Hill's Keys to Success: The Seventeen
 Principles of Personal Achievement*, edited by
 Matthew Sartwell
*1001 Reasons to Think Positive: Special Insights
 to Achieve a Better Attitude Toward Life*, Ella
 Patterson
The Prophet, Kahlil Gibran
The Prosperity Secret of the Ages, Catherine
 Ponder
Random Acts of Kindness, editors of Conari
 Press
The Road Less Traveled, M. Scott Peck

The Seven Habits of Highly Effective People,
 Stephen R. Covey
The Sky's the Limit, Wayne W. Dyer
*Success is Not an Accident: The Mental Bank
 Concept*, John G. Kappas
When Bad Things Happen to Good People, Harold
 S. Kushner

ETIQUETTE

The Amy Vanderbilt Complete Book of Etiquette,
 Nancy Tuckerman and Nancy Dunnan
*Elements of Etiquette: A Guide to Table Manners
 in an Imperfect World*, Craig Claiborne
Emily Post's Etiquette, Peggy Post
*Etiquette in Society, in Business, in Politics, and
 at Home*, Emily Post
*Letitia Baldridge's Complete Guide to the New
 Manners for the 90's*, Letitia Baldrige
*Miss Manners' Guide for the Turn-of-the-
 Millenium*, Judith Martin
*The New Etiquette: Real Manners for Real People
 in Real Situations*, Marjabelle Young Stewart

I also suggest purchasing books on business
growth, human psychology and any books on
trends. Also, look into your regional community
for local networking directories that list different organizations and clubs within your town or
community. With the thousands of books available to you, there is no excuse for not networking effectively or for lacking in your business
and communication skills.

The activity on the World Wide Web is also
a tremendous way to build your library; they
advertise the latest and greatest in all resource
materials, especially books. The Internet, is the
future, so make good use of it as you gather
materials for your library.

Epilogue

As I said at the beginning of this book, networking is an activity that enables you to access and link up to appropriate and useful connections. And the "activity" of it all can take many shapes and forms. There is no one way to network. By combining a variety of skills—your ability to research, reach out for contacts and communicate positively with others—you will lay solid groundwork to forge and capitalize on lifelong relationships. It is those very relationships that will sustain you and help you grow throughout the rest of your professional life.

In closing, one of the most important messages I wish to impart to you is that networking is never ending. Make your networking activities part of your daily regime. What you put into networking is exactly what you'll get out of it.

Don't forget that your resource center—your carefully assembled database—is something you will use for the rest of your professional life. Let it build on itself, and be sure to keep it up-to-date.

Pay close attention to your communication skills and how to relate to others. Take good care of your contacts, and consistently present yourself professionally.

Networking takes a great deal of effort and stamina, creativity, perseverance and resolve, and I ask that you take a moment to bask in the glow of all the hard work you've done thus far.

The assignments in this book took a great deal of introspection, exploration and willingness to knock down walls to reach your custom-tailored destinations. But you did it, and for that you should be proud.

In that same spirit, don't forget to stop and acknowledge your efforts along the way. Find a "networking anniversary date," and each year, itemize and review the progress you've made from the prior year. When networking seems arduous, take time out to tally your accomplishments and measure the distance from your original starting point. You'll be amazed at how far you've come.

So before you step forward into the vast world

of networking, take a moment to congratulate yourself for all the new skills you acquired as you worked your way through this book. Continue to be generous with compliments to yourself; they will provide a great deal of motivation, especially on those days when it's hard to keep plugging away.

There are days when I ask myself: "Is it worth it?" The answer is always a resounding "yes" because I can see that my time has been well spent. Just one new contact reiterates the importance and need for me to stay in the loop.

If you ever feel stuck as you aspire to get ahead, go back and review your worksheets. Tap into all your resources, and call upon your mentors and advisors when you need them.

Enjoy the results of all your hard work thus far and all the benefits that lie ahead as you network your way to the job you want.

But one last and most important thing of all: Always think in terms of establishing, maintaining and nurturing relationships. In the end, that's the heart and soul of what networking is all about.

INDEX